The Vampire & His Pleasant Companions

2

MARIMO RAGAWA

ORIGINAL STORY
NARISE KONOHARA

ACT 5
THE FIRST TASTE OF CHOICE RED

CONTENTS

ZUKIN (PANG)
OW.
ZUKIN
IT HURTS.
ZUKIN
IT HURTS...
WHAT...WAS THAT?
ZAAA (FWSHHH
HE ACTUALLY TRIED TO KILL ME...?
HFF...

WELL, HE'S AN IDIOT.
I'M A VAMPIRE, SO I'M NOT GONNA DIE.
SUCKS TO BE HIM.
!!
BUSHI (SPLURT)
MY WOUNDS AREN'T HEALING VERY QUICKLY.
I FEEL WEAK.
I'M COLD.
GACHI GACHI GACHI (CHATTER)
ガチ ガチ ガチ
IF THIS KEEPS UP, THERE'S NO TELLING HOW LONG IT'LL BE BEFORE I CAN MOVE AGAIN.
ZAAA (FWSHHH)

ZAAAA
BISHA (SPLISH)
BISHA
SOMEBODY'S HERE.
I'M SLEEPY.
PASHA (SPLASH)
PASHA
BA (TPP)
BA
BA
BA
BA
BA
PASHA
IS IT THAT GUY AGAIN?

DID HE COME BACK...
ハロ
PASHA (SPLASH)
...TO FINISH ME OFF?
ビシャ
BISHA (SPLISH)
ビシャ
BISHA
IS THAT...
...AKIRA...
...MAYBE...?
ザ
ZAAA (FWSHHH)

BASHA (SPLASH)
BASHA
ZAAA
I SURE HOPE IT'S AKIRA.
A...
A...
...KI...
...RA...

IT'S AKIRA.
HE CAME.

ZAAA (FWSHHH)
ザ
HOW THE HELL DID THIS HAPPEN!?
AKIRA...
NO GET MAD...
FORGET JAPANESE! SPEAK ENGLISH!!
BESHA (SPLAT)
ベシャッ
A GUY STABBED ME.
WHO!?
DUNNO. NEVER EVEN SEEN HIM BEFORE.
ZO (SHUDDER)
ゾッ
LOOK...
...ARE YOU GOING TO BE OKAY? THIS IS JUST...
I'M OKAY.

I'M...
...NOT NORMAL.
I'LL HEAL UP FAST.
......
OVER IN AMERICA, I WAS BASICALLY HOMELESS, SO I'VE RUN INTO LOTS OF NASTY STUFF.
Ouch!
DON'T SCREW WITH ME LIKE THIS.
YOU STUPID IDIOT. WHAT IF YOU'D DIED?
NO WORRIES THERE.

I DON'T DIE.
AFTER THAT...
...FOR THREE DAYS...
...I SLEPT WITHOUT WAKING.
MY WOUNDS HEALED COMPLETELY, AND YET...
...I FEEL WEAK...
...I CAN'T GET UP.
I DON'T HAVE ENOUGH BLOOD.
HEALING THOSE WOUNDS DRAINED ALL MY ENERGY.

HEY.
YOU'VE HEALED...
...SO WHY CAN'T YOU MOVE?
MY STRENGTH...
...DOWN.
I'M GIVING YOU TRIPLE THE CHICKEN LIVERS. YOU EVEN GET STEAK.
I EAT.
STRENGTH ...
...CHARGE UP.
IT OKAY.

......
AKIRA'S KIND.
DURING THE WORST OF THE PAIN, HE RUBBED MY BACK THE WHOLE TIME.
SO EVEN IF MY STRENGTH DOESN'T COME BACK, I DON'T MIND...
COULD IT BE...
IS EVEN STEAK NOT NUTRITIOUS ENOUGH FOR YOU?
DOKI (BADMP)
SINCE YOUR WOUNDS HEALED, I THOUGHT YOU WERE FINE, BUT... YOU DID LOSE A TON OF BLOOD.
SORT OF. BUT...
...I HANDLE.
OKAY.

TODAY, YOU'RE GETTING A FEAST.
ガタ
GATA (CLATTER)
ガチャ ガチャ
GACHA (CLINK) GACHA
...FEAST...? A...
パチーンッ
PACHIN (SNAP)
I HAVE TOMORROW OFF.
I'LL GIVE YOU SOME OF MY BLOOD. JUST A LITTLE. JUST THIS ONCE.
ドクッ
DOKU (BADMP)
WHAT... IS HE...?
ス
SU (POKE)
WHA...?

ドクン
DOKUN
THE TERMS ARE...
グ
GU (TUG)
パチン
PACHIN
...NO MORE THAN 400CC.
DON'T WASTE A DROP.
ドクン
DOKUN
ドクン
DOKUN

GET A MOVE ON!
IT'S DRIPPING.
ドクン
DOKUN
ドクン
DOKUN (BADMP)
I'VE...
...NEVER TAKEN...
NOT EVEN...
...ONCE.
クラッ
KURA (DIZZY)
...HUMAN BLOOD.

DO
(FOOM)

WA
(FOOSH)
GU
(SQUEEZE)
WHAT...
...IS...
...THIS?
IT'S
FANTASTIC!!
GHK!

じゅっ
JYU (SLURP)
DELICIOUS.
HEY!
CONTROL YOURSELF!
GU (SHOVE)
グッ
LOOK...
...YOU—!
R—
REMEMBER WHAT I SAID!?
GUGUGU (STRAIN)
グググ
UH-OH. I'M HOOKED.

CHUUUU (SUCK)
ちゅううう
ENOUGH!
HEY!
NKU (GULP)
NKU
NKU
SERI-OUSLY...
WOULD YOU KNOCK IT...
GO (WHUNK)
GO
...OFF!?
FU (PALE)
AH...
"AH"?

ふ〜らぁ
FURAAAA (TOTTER)
あ
あー
AH.
AKI-RAAA!?
バターン
BATAAAN (FWUMP)
ドドドーン
DON (BAM)
DON
DON
ピポピポピポーン
PIPON
PIPON (DING-DONG)
PIPON
WHAT, DAM-MIT!?
SHUT THE HELL U—
ガチャ
GACHA (GACHAK)
UHH...
UH.
?

バッ
BA (LUNGE)
HELP!!
I THINK HE'S GONNA DIE!! CALL AN AMBULANCE!
WAAAH!!
ガッ
GA (GRAB)
BLOOD
MY FRIEND IS GONNA DIE!!
NAKED
AMBULANCE! STAT!
YEEEEEEG!
I—
I DON'T SPEAK ENGLISH!!
THERE'S NOTHING VALUABLE IN HERE, I SWEAR!!
パパパパ
PA (WHAP)
PA
PA
PA
パーンッ
PAN
JAPA...
...NESE...

GA
AM...
...BU...
...LANCE!
CALL!
CALL FOR HIM!
HELP MY FRIEND!
PLEASE!
PLEASE!

HE'S ANEMIC AND DEHYDRATED.
AND THE MAN WHO CAME WITH HIM?
YOU SAY HE ONLY SPEAKS BROKEN JAPANESE?
WHAT DO I DO...?
WHAT AM I GONNA DO IF AKIRA DIES?
HE WAS GIVING ME BLOOD...
HE'S A TOTAL TYRANT, AND HE'S SURLY AND MOUTHY, AND HE HITS, BUT...
HEY.
OH, AND HE'S VINDICTIVE TOO, BUT...
LOOK, YOU...
...I'VE STARTED TO SEE THAT HE'S REALLY A KIND GUY, AND YET...
EXCUSE ME.
HOW ARE YOU RELATED TO THE PATIENT?
I'M HIS FRIEND.

IN THAT CASE, DO YOU KNOW HOW TO CONTACT HIS FAMILY?
!?
DO (BADMP)
IS HE GOING TO DIE?
HUH...? NO... THAT'S NOT... WHY I'M...
SHIRT: PROVIDING MORE MEMORIES THAN THE HEART CAN HOLD / OLD MEMORIAL CENTER
IF AKIRA DIES, MY LIFE WILL BE OVER TOO.
I SEE...
UU! GH!
NNH!
HE TOLD ME TO STOP, BUT I...
MM-HM...
I JUST COULDN'T CONTROL MYSELF.
I SEE...
I COULDN'T STOP...
...AND HIS BODY JUST COULDN'T TAKE IT...

CREAK
DOCTOR ITOU, THE PATIENT IS AWAKE NOW.
HE'S RESPONSIVE.
IT SOUNDS AS IF HE'S REGAINED CONSCIOUSNESS.
HUH?
BY THE WAY, HE'S SERIOUSLY ANEMIC, BUT THERE ARE NO EXTERNAL WOUNDS.
HE MAY BE BLEEDING INTERNALLY.
CAN YOU TELL US ANYTHING ABOUT THAT?
......
DOKI (BADMP) ドキ・ドキ DOKI
THEY CAN'T KNOW I'M A VAMPIRE, CAN THEY...?
IF YOU'D RATHER NOT SAY, WE WON'T FORCE YOU.
PLEASE TAKE CARE OF HIM.
PEKO (BOW) ペコッ
語り
思
PICHI (SNAP) ピチッ
TOKA-SHIKI-SAN!
YES!
READY THE ANO-SCOPE!!

ACCORDING TO HIS PARTNER OUTSIDE...
...IT SOUNDS LIKE THEY WERE HAVING SOME PRETTY HARD-CORE FUN.
I'LL HAVE TO INSPECT EVERY NOOK AND CRANNY TO MAKE SURE WE DON'T MISS ANYTHING!!
TAKATSUKA-SAAAN. WE'RE GOING TO EXAMINE YOU NOW.
HUH?
WHAT?
THIS MAY BE A LITTLE UNCOMFORTABLE, BUT I NEED YOU TO LIE ON YOUR SIDE, PLEASE.
JUST RELAX, OKAY?
"EVERY NOOK" ...?
I THOUGHT IT WAS ANEMIA.
CORRECT!!
SERIOUS ANEMIA, WITH NO EXTERNAL WOUNDS...
...AND NO ABNORMAL READINGS!!
WE CAN'T RISK OVERLOOKING AN INTERNAL TEAR!!

NEXT TIME...
GIRAAAN (GLINT)
ギラーン
...TELL YOUR FRIEND OUTSIDE TO GO EASIER ON YOU!!
SIGN: AKAGAKI HOSPITAL
GUNYUUU (SQUISH)
ぐにゅううっ
赤垣病院
AKIRA.
KON (TAP)
コン
YOU ALIVE?

GIRORI (GLARE)
ギロリッ
SHIRT: FUNERAL HOME
HOW DID YOU KNOW I WAS HERE? DID THIS IDIOT CALL YOU?
NO.
I STOPPED BY YOUR PLACE AFTER WORK.
THE DOOR WAS UNLOCKED, THE ROOM WAS A MESS, AND THERE WAS A BLOODY TOWEL...
WHEN I ASKED YOUR NEIGHBOR, HE SAID YOU'D BEEN TAKEN AWAY BY AMBULANCE.
I'M IMPRESSED THEY LET YOU IN HERE AT THIS HOUR.
WELL, YOU KNOW. DETECTIVE'S PRIVILEGE.
SO? WHAT ON EARTH HAPPENED?
IT'S THIS IDIOT'S FAULT.
?
I GAVE HIM SOME OF MY BLOOD...
...AND HE JUST KEPT GUZZLING IT. I ALMOST DIED.
BLOOD?

I AM SORRY.
I NOT...
...STOP.
HEAD...
...KNOW.
BUT BODY...
...NOT KNOW.
I AM SORRY.
YOU WERE WEAK, AND I FELT BAD FOR YOU.
I SYMPATHIZED, AND THIS IS WHAT I GET.
ON TOP OF THAT, THEY THINK IT WAS GAY SEX THAT GOT TOO ROUGH.
WHAT THE HELL DID YOU TELL THAT DOCTOR!?
I NOT SAY YOU G AY.
IF YOU DIDN'T SAY IT, WHO DID!?
GRAH!
I AM...
...SORRY.
I GET THE GIST OF WHAT HAPPENED.
LOOK, AL REGRETS WHAT HE DID.
NADE (PAT)
なで
HE THINKS I'LL FORGIVE HIM IF HE APOLOGIZES!

I'VE BEEN TOO BUSY TO COME BY LATELY.
HAVE YOU NOT BEEN FEELING SO GOOD, AL?
I...
...NO ABLE WAKE UP.
KOKU (NOD)
こく
YOU CAN USE ENGLISH WITH ME.
AKIRA.
HE CAN'T EXPLAIN PROPERLY IN JAPANESE.
GRR...
THREE DAYS AGO...
...I GOT STABBED. WITH A KNIFE.
WHAT!? BY AKIRA!?
WHY WOULD I DO THAT!?
NO.
I WAS IN THE PARK, AND SOME RANDOM GUY I'D NEVER SEEN BEFORE STABBED ME IN THE BACK.
思い出を

WHAT THE GUY DID TO AL AT THE PARK...
...AND SO ON, AND SO FORTH...
BUT...
...THAT'S A MAJOR INCIDENT!!
AKIRA!! WHY DIDN'T YOU TELL ME ABOUT THIS!?
...OH. WELL, HIS WOUNDS HEALED UP.
I FORGOT HE'D GOTTEN THEM FROM SOMEBODY ELSE.
AL SURVIVED BECAUSE HE'S A VAMPIRE. A HUMAN WOULD HAVE DIED.
WE CAN'T LET A GUY WHO'D DO A THING LIKE THAT WALK FREE! IT'S DANGEROUS!
I REALLY WISH YOU'D TOLD ME WHEN AL GOT HURT.
I DIDN'T THINK THAT FAR.
I'M SORRY.

AKIRA CAN'T STAND UP TO NUKARIYA.
BY THE WAY, WOULD YOU TAKE THIS IDIOT BACK HOME?
HEH HEH HEH...
YOU'RE IN THE WAY! GO HOME!!
HOME?
NO! I STAY.
STAY WITH YOU.
HE'S RIGHT, AL.
A.M. BAT
IF THERE'S A BAT HERE IN THE MORNING, THE WHOLE HOSPITAL WILL BE IN AN UPROAR.
AH!
BESIDES, THE APARTMENT'S STILL UNLOCKED.
GO HOME!!
A...
AKI RA.
I...
...NOTHING TO BUY.
VAMPIRE...
NOT EAT. NOT DRINK.

BODY...
NOT... NO RM...? NORMAL.
NO THING TO BUY.
I SAD.
THREE DAYS BEFORE, YOU GET MAD.
I AM... SORRY.
ALL RIGHT.

PHEW.
DON'T HANG OVER ME LIKE THAT.
IT'S DARK.
GAAAN (SHOCK)
YOU'RE IN THE WAY.
GO HOME ALREADY.
HE'LL ONLY BE HOSPITALIZED OVERNIGHT. DON'T WORRY.
OKAY, AKIRA.
TAKE CARE.
HEY!
ALSO, I FOUND YOUR KEY AND LOCKED UP BEFORE I CAME, SO YOU'RE SAFE THERE.
PATAN (SHUT)
HAAH...
THAT IDIOT.
SO IT'S MY FAULT, HUH?

AL.
THERE HAVE BEEN STABBINGS IN THE AREA RECENTLY.
DID YOU KNOW ABOUT THEM?
EVEN IF I WATCH THE NEWS, I DON'T UNDERSTAND IT.
I SEE...
SIGN: RECEPTION FOR RETURNING PATIENTS
SINCE LAST MONTH, TWO PEOPLE HAVE BEEN KILLED IN THE SAME WAY.
BOTH WERE STABBED IN THE STOMACH AND BACK WITH A KNIFE, THEN HAD THEIR THROATS CUT.
ZO (SHUDDER)
THAT SOUNDS LIKE WHAT HAPPENED TO YOU, DOESN'T IT?

IF YOU WEREN'T A VAMPIRE...
...YOU COULD HAVE BEEN THE THIRD VICTIM.
I SEE.
MY WOUNDS HEAL UP FAST, SO...
...I DIDN'T GIVE MUCH THOUGHT TO WHAT THAT STABBING MEANT.
WILL THE GUY DO IT AGAIN?
HE'LL PROBABLY KEEP DOING IT UNTIL HE GETS CAUGHT.
AL.
WILL YOU COOPERATE WITH OUR INVESTIGATION?

THERE'S A VERY GOOD CHANCE THAT YOUR ATTACKER IS THE KILLER.
IF WE CAN CATCH HIM, THERE WON'T HAVE TO BE ANOTHER VICTIM.
ZAWA (SHIVER)
ザワッ
KYU (CLENCH)
きゅっ
BE USEFUL... TO OTHERS?
ME?
EVER SINCE I ENDED UP LIKE THIS, I'VE BEEN TREATED LIKE A BURDEN, BUT...
AL?

I'LL...
...COOPERATE.
THAT GUY'S THE KILLER FOR SURE.
HE WAS LAUGHING WHILE HE STABBED ME.
HE SAID SOMETHING LIKE, "HURRY UP AND DIE."
IT'S NOT OKAY TO SAY STUFF LIKE THAT TO PEOPLE.
SO GET HIM.

BOFUN (FWUMP)
ぼふんっ
I'M ALL BETTER NOW.
I SHOULDN'T SLEEP IN THE BED ANYMORE.
I FEEL LIKE I'M OVERFLOWING WITH POWER.

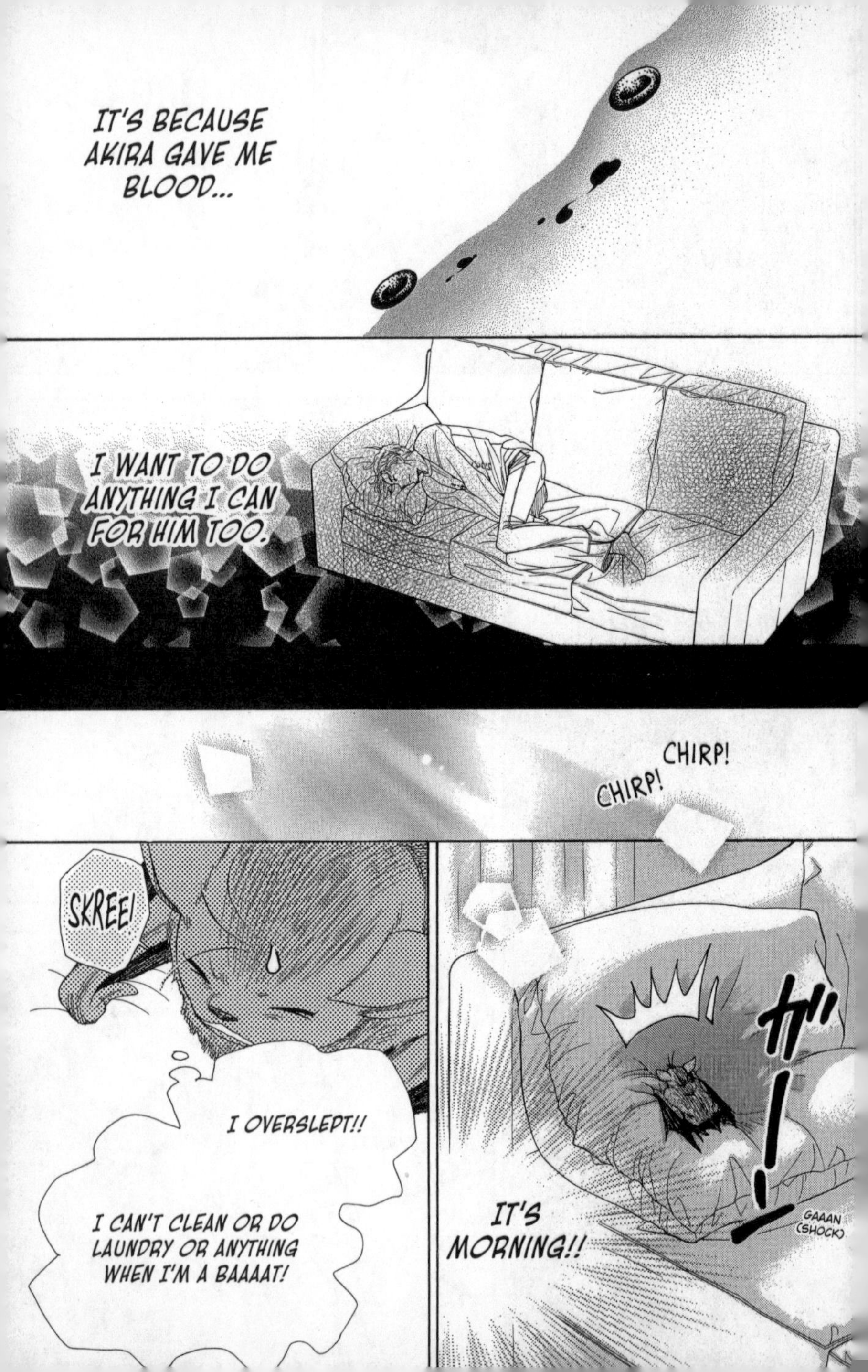
IT'S BECAUSE AKIRA GAVE ME BLOOD...
I WANT TO DO ANYTHING I CAN FOR HIM TOO.
CHIRP!
CHIRP!
GAAAN (SHOCK)
IT'S MORNING!!
SKREE!
I OVERSLEPT!!
I CAN'T CLEAN OR DO LAUNDRY OR ANYTHING WHEN I'M A BAAAAT!

TICK
TICK
TICK
TICK
I WONDER WHEN AKIRA'S COMING HOME.
MON (FRET) MON
もんもん
うつうつ
UTSU UTSU (MOPE)
UUU~~
I CAN'T GO VISIT HIM EITHER.
KACHI (KACHAK)
カチ
GACHA (RATTLE)
ガチャ
GACHA
ガチャ
HAH!
SKREE!
SKREE!
SHUT UP!
SKREE!
SKREE! SKREE!
BASA (FLAP)
バサ
SKREE!
BASA
バサ
YOU'RE GIVING ME A HEAD-ACHE!

MMF!
ガチャ
GACHA
バサッ
BASA
バサッ
BASA (FWAP)
チャ
CHA (CHAK)
キュッ
KYU (SQUEAK)
ジャー
SHAAA (FWSSSH)
....
はぐっ
HAGU (NOMF)
I'LL PUT THIS...
...OVER IN THE CORNER, AT LEAST.
ぐっ
GU (TUG)
GU
GU

PIRI (RIP)
GACHA (KACHAK)
HM?
WHAT WAS THAT NOISE?
BIKU (FLINCH)
BOTARI (PLOP)
HEY.
WHAT WERE YOU D—
PIKI (IRK)
Close-up
YOU DAMN BAT!
WHAT DID YOU JUST DO!?

YEEEP...
I'VE HAD ONE HELL OF A TIME THANKS TO YOU!!
DON'T DO ANYTHING THAT'S GOING TO MAKE ME MADDER!!
フラ...
FURA (SWAY)
!?
ぼふんっ
BOFUN (FLUMP)

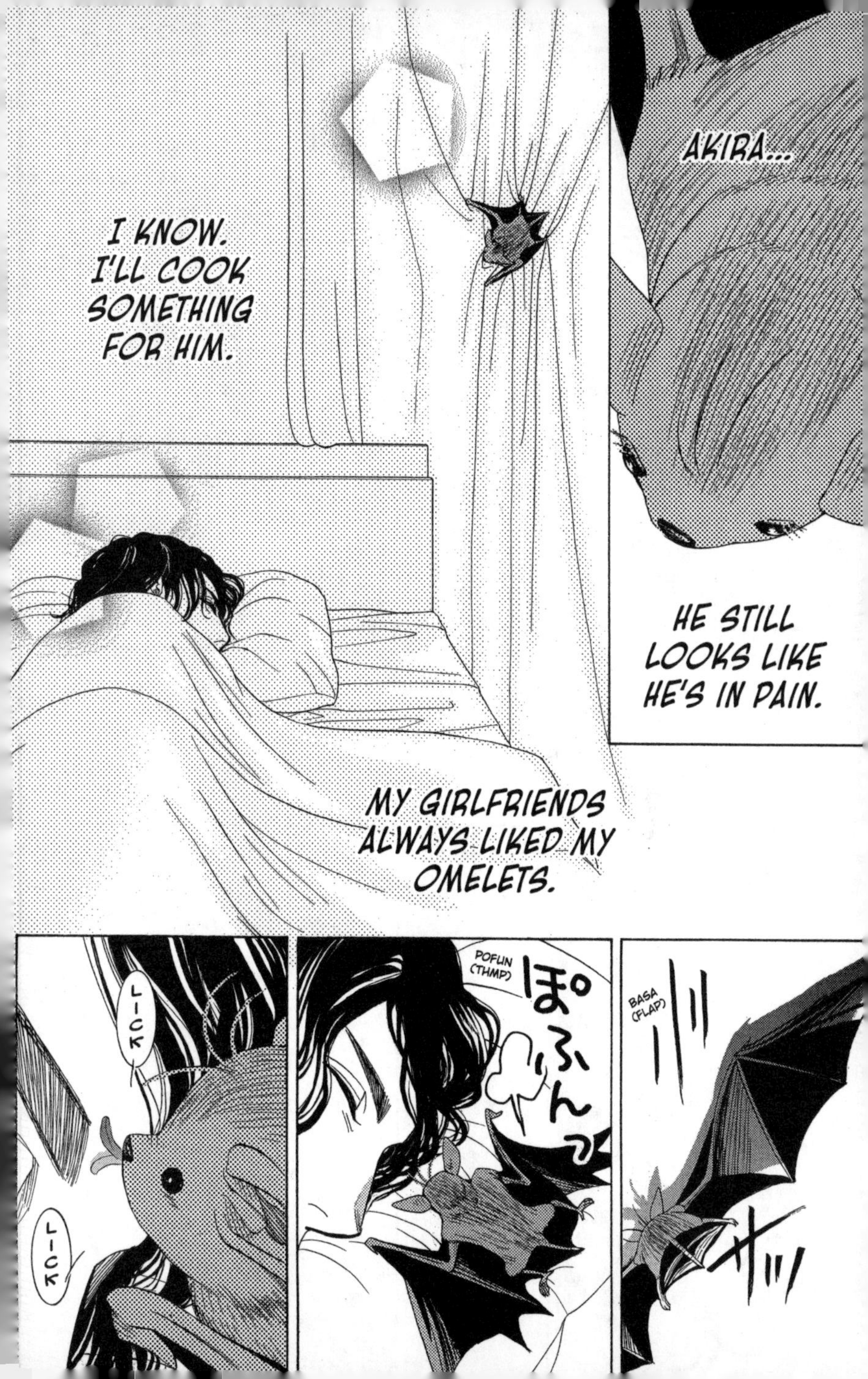

AKIRA...
HE STILL LOOKS LIKE HE'S IN PAIN.
I KNOW. I'LL COOK SOMETHING FOR HIM.
MY GIRLFRIENDS ALWAYS LIKED MY OMELETS.
BASA (FLAP)
POFUN (THMP)
ぽふんっ
LICK
LICK

HMPH.
GISHI (CREAK)
ギシ

SURI (NUZZLE)
スリ
I WONDER...
ZZZ...
ZZZ...
...IF WE HAVE EGGS IN THE FRIDGE...

ACT 6 | EMBALMER
IT'S PITCH BLACK.
IT'S WAY TOO CRAMPED.
WHERE AM I?
LEMME OUT!!
LET ME OUT OF HERE!!
GAKO (CLUNK)

HFF!
HFF!
HFF!
HFF!
ALBERT IRVING
APPARENTLY, I DIED.

ACT 6 | EMBALMER

SO WHERE SHOULD I HAVE GONE?
MOM!! IT'S ME.
IT'S ALBERT—AL!!
Who's there, at this hour!?
You brought a boy with a voice like my son's!? You're awful!!
That's impossible! You're a burglar, aren't you!!?
That's not funny!!
AWFUL? NO...!
TRUST ME!
I'M AL! I'LL PROVE IT!
IT'S TRUE! I CAME BACK TO LIFE...
OPEN THE DOOR AND LOOK AT ME!!

THREE CHRISTMASES AGO, YOU GAVE ME A BLUE SWEATER.
Just stop!
Stop it!!
Don't say anything else!!
WHEN I WAS FIFTEEN, I GOT HURT IN A SOCCER GAME AND WAS SENT TO THE HOSPITAL, AND YOU CAME FLYING BACK FROM GRANDMA'S HOUSE IN OKLAHOMA.
PAN (BANG)
WHEN I BROUGHT GIRLFRIENDS HOME FROM COLLEGE...
...YOU SAID YOU LIKED JAHNE, BUT YOU REALLY WEREN'T A FAN OF AMMALINE.
THE JEWELRY YOU BOUGHT WITHOUT TELLING DAD IS HIDDEN IN THE BACK OF THE SIDEBOARD, ON THE RIGHT!!
D...DAD...

GET THE HELL OUT OF HERE, DEMON-SPAWN!!
PAN (BANG)
PAN
PAN
BAN (BAM)
BAN
GREG!
IT'S ME! ALBERT! OPEN UP!
AAAH!

JUST LISTEN TO ME!
WHEN I CAME TO, I WAS IN A COFFIN...
MY FOLKS DON'T BELIEVE I CAME BACK TO LIFE!!
TH-THERE'S NO WAY YOU DID!
I SAW YOUR DEAD BODY, DUDE!!
YOU WERE JUST SKIN AND BONES, AND YOU LOOKED LIKE AN OLD GEEZER.
BUT AT THE FUNERAL, YOUR FACE WAS FILLED OUT AGAIN. YOU LOOKED GOOD.
YOUR MOM SAID THEY'D MANAGED TO GET A GOOD EMBALMER. SHE WAS CRYING...
I MEAN, C'MON, THERE'S NO WAY YOU COULD COME BACK AFTER THAT!!
I WAS YOUR BEST FRIEND! WHY ARE YOU HAUNTING ME!?

YOU DIED!!
BUT I DIDN'T HAVE ANYWHERE TO GO.
BEHAVE AND PASS ON, ALL RIGHT!?
OVERWHELMING THIRST AND HUNGER FLOODED ME.
I DRANK WATER IN SOMEBODY'S YARD, BUT IT DIDN'T HELP AT ALL.
SOMETHING WAS PHYSICALLY WRONG WITH ME.
I DIDN'T KNOW WHAT OR WHERE...
...BUT SOMETHING WAS OFF.

AND THEN...
...WHEN THE MORNING SUN PEEKED OVER THE HORIZON...
...THE WORLD TURNED BLACK AND WHITE, LIKE AN OLD MOVIE.
I...
...WAS A BAT.

IT'S ALREADY BEEN EIGHT YEARS SINCE THEN.
ZAWA (MURMUR)
ザワ
COFFEE
ZAWA
ザワ
DOES THIS LOOK ABOUT RIGHT?
AL...
...THANK YOU FOR YOUR COOPERATION.
IT'S FINE.
IF IT'LL HELP YOU CATCH THAT GUY, I'LL DO ANYTHING.
YEAH.

BETTER BEWARE.
HEH HEH HEH!
NUKARIYA-CHAN LOOKS LIKE A NICE GUY, BUT HE'S A REAL SLAVE DRIVER.
OKAY, I'LL GO TURN THIS IN.
THANKS.
"BEWARE"?
"SLAVE DRIVER"?
カラ
KARA (EMPTY)
......
BY THE WAY, AL...
?
....
OH... NEVER MIND. IT'S NOTHING.
?
NUKA-RIYA... YOU A WEIRDO.
AH-HA-HA.
HOW LONG HAVE YOU BEEN HERE, A MONTH? YOUR JAPANESE IS GETTING BETTER.
WE'RE BACK.

ARE YOU DONE HELPING WITH THE INVESTIGATION, OR WHATEVER IT WAS?
YEAH.
NUKARIYA COME WITH ME.
PARDON THE INTRUSION.
I'LL BE HEADING BACK TO WORK SOON.
HEY!
YOU ATE RAMEN!?
I MADE FOOD!
WHERE IT GO!?
LIKE I COULD EAT THAT STUFF!?
I BET YOU THINK THE CALORIES ARE ALL THAT MATTER.
NO!! WHEN I MAKE, YUMMY!
PRETTY!
ばいんっ
BAIN (BOING)

YOU CAN COOK, AL?
LEARNING.
YOU EAT IT, THEN.
HE WENT TO THE TROUBLE OF MAKING IT FOR YOU. IT'S BAD LUCK NOT TO EAT IT.
CHOCOLATE-FLAVORED MISO SOUP AND SASHIMI WITH KETCHUP AND MUSTARD ON THE SIDE.
URP.
I...
...LEARN LOTS AND...
...LOTS.
I BE...
...USE-FUL.
TO AKIRA.
......
NIKO
NIKO (SMILE)
IF YOU'RE GOING TO LIVE IN JAPAN, LEARN FOR YOUR OWN SAKE.
IT'S A MILLION YEARS TOO SOON FOR YOU TO BE USEFUL TO ME.
OF COURSE!!
I LEARN FOR ME.

BUT!
I...
...LIKE AKIRA.
AND SO...
...I BE USEFUL!!
FLATTERY WILL GET YOU NOWHERE.
HUH? WHAT THAT MEAN?
"USING FAKE COMPLIMENTS TO PUT SOMEONE IN A GOOD MOOD."
NOT FLATTERY.
NO!!
OH DEAR...
WAH!
GABA (POUNCE)

I LIKE YOU.
FOR REAL.
GO (WHUNK)
YOU WANT TO BE USEFUL!? THEN HURRY AND CLEAN UP THAT REVOLTING STUFF YOU MADE!!
UUUU!
"RE-BOLTING"...?
AND?
DID YOU NEED SOMETHING?

MM...
TO BE HONEST, I THOUGHT AL WASN'T LOOKING SO GOOD.
EVEN IF I ASK HIM, HE'LL PROBABLY SAY HE'S FINE BECAUSE HE DOESN'T WANT TO WORRY YOU.
HE DID LOSE A LOT OF BLOOD RECENTLY. IF IT'S ALL RIGHT WITH YOU, I'LL BRING HIM SOME BEEF.
カチャ KACHA (CLINK)
カチャ KACHA
OH!
HE SCRAPED OFF THE KETCHUP AND ATE THE FISH.
くぅ KUU (GURGLE)
ぐるるるる〜 GURURURU (RRRUMBLE)
ぐー GUUU (GRRRGL)
きゅるるる KYURURURU (RRRRMBL)
ARGH. I'M HUNGRY.
THE EFFECT OF AKIRA'S BLOOD IS JUST ABOUT GONE.
WHEN I WAS AT JAN'S FACTORY, I WAS MOST ACTIVE AS A BAT...
...BUT HERE, I MOVE AROUND MORE WHILE I'M HUMAN...

STILL...
...THIS IS THE MOST "HUMAN" LIFE I'VE LIVED IN AGES.
EVER SINCE I FOUND OUT I'D BECOME A VAMPIRE...
GOOD EVENING.
ARE THERE ANY TASTY YOUNG THINGS AROUND HERE?

HIS NAME WAS KIEV.
HE'D BEEN A VAMPIRE FOR ABOUT THREE HUNDRED YEARS.
WELL, WELL...
YOU RAN INTO A RATHER UNHINGED YOUNG LADY.
ORDINARILY, WHEN WE TAKE BLOOD, WE KEEP IT TO NONFATAL AMOUNTS.
SHE MUST HAVE EITHER BEEN VERY NEW AND UNABLE TO CONTROL HERSELF...
...OR EXTREMELY ANNOYED.
DOESN'T EVERYBODY TURN INTO A VAMPIRE IF YOU DRINK THEIR BLOOD?
PERISH THE THOUGHT.

IF THAT WERE THE CASE, THE WORLD WOULD BE CRAWLING WITH VAMPIRES.
TO TURN A HUMAN INTO ONE OF US, YOU HAVE TO DRINK THEIR BLOOD UNTIL THEY DIE.
......
BY THE WAY...
...I'VE BEEN WONDERING ABOUT IT FOR A WHILE NOW.
WHY ARE YOU LETTING YOURSELF GO HUNGRY?
NOTHING COULD BE SIMPLER THAN DRINKING BLOOD.

PURURU (RRRING)
プルルル
AH!
YES, THIS IS TAKATSUKA.
WHAT?
YOU MEAN NOW?
WHAT ABOUT KOYANAGI-SAN? ...HE CAN'T?
YES.
ALL RIGHT.
PHONE: OLD MEMORIAL
モリアル
ト
TO (TAP)
A JOB?
YEAH.
AFTER YOU STOPPED BY AND EVERYTHING. I'M SORRY.
DON'T WORRY ABOUT IT. I'LL HEAD BACK TO THE STATION.

AL.
I'M GOING OUT.
NOW?
MM-HMM. NOW.
IT'S WORK.
DON'T WAIT UP.
LOCK THE FRONT DOOR BEFORE YOU TURN IN.
IF THEY CALLED YOU IN AT THIS HOUR, IT MUST BE A REAL EMERGENCY.
THE BODY IS BEING LOADED ONTO AN INTERNATIONAL FLIGHT FIRST THING TOMORROW.
IT'S A FOREIGNER?
YEAH.
THEY SAID HE'S GOING HOME TO RWANDA.
AT THIS HOUR, I WON'T HAVE AN ASSISTANT EITHER.
I HOPE I FINISH IN TIME, BUT...
ASSISTANT...
ASSIST. HELP OUT.

AKIRA!
I...
...HELP OUT!
I HELP!
THIS IS AN IMPORTANT JOB AKIRA DOES FOR SOMEBODY ELSE.
QUIT JOKING AROUND!!
IT'S NOT A JOB AN AMATEUR COULD HELP WITH!!
I WANT TO DO SOMETHING FOR AKIRA!!
I DO WHAT YOU SAY.
JUST LIKE YOU SAY.

YOU'LL BE IN THE WAY!!
NOT BE IN WAY.
I SWEAR.
AL.
AKIRA'S JOB REQUIRES TECHNICAL SKILLS. I DON'T THINK YOU COULD HELP.
I BE USEFUL!
GASHI (GRAB)
I DO ANYTHING!!
TAKE ME TOO!!

—I'VE FELT THIS...BEFORE.
LIKE HELL.
...HE SAID.
HE HELD ME BACK.
...OH.
HAAAH...
THERE'S NOT MUCH TIME BEFORE THAT FIRST FLIGHT.
DON'T DO A THING EXCEPT WHAT I TELL YOU.

GOOD FOR YOU.
GO GIVE IT YOUR BEST.
Y— YEAH!
YEAH.
SIGN: OLD MEMORIAL CENTER
I'LL GIVE THIS...
...ALL I'VE GOT.
オールドメモリアル センター

KON (TAP)
MATSUMURA-SAN. DO YOU HAVE THE PAPERS?
TAKA-TSUKA-KUN.
YOU GOT HERE QUICKLY.
I'M SORRY TO CALL YOU IN SO SUDDENLY.
YOU HANDLED THE LAST EMERGENCY...
...SO I CALLED KOYANAGI-KUN THIS TIME...
...BUT HIS WIFE'S IN BED WITH A COLD, AND HE HAS HIS HANDS FULL OVER THERE.
YOU KNOW.
THEY HAVE TWO CHILDREN, AFTER ALL.
PARA (FLIP)
OH...AKIRA'S IGNORING HER?
HARA (FRET)
HARA

CHIRA (GLANCE)
チラ
GOOD EVENING.
ニコリ
NIKORI (SMILE)
MY, HE'S HANDSOME.
GOOD EVENING. YOUR JAPANESE IS VERY GOOD.
I LEARNING.
LISTENING OKAY.
NO SPEAK YET.
I'VE LOOKED THROUGH THE PAPERWORK. PRETTY SURE I'LL BE ABLE TO FINISH UP IN THREE HOURS.
BY THE WAY, WHO IS HE?
ニコ
NIKO (SMILE)
HE'S OB-SERVING.
ニコ
NIKO
AT THIS HOUR?
DOES HE WANT TO BE AN EMBALMER?
SOMETHING LIKE THAT.
LET'S GO.
OH... UH-HUH.

PUT THESE ON.
バサ
BASA (RUSTLE)
わた
WATA
わた
WATA (FLAIL)
OH!
UH!

PATA (PATTER)
PATA
LISTEN UP.
I'M TELLING YOU THIS UP FRONT.
ONCE WE WALK THROUGH THIS DOOR...
...DON'T TALK TO ME.
NO MATTER WHAT.

こく
KOKU (NOD)
ウィーンッ
UIN (VREEN)

DOKUN (BADMP)
ドクン
DOKUN
ドクン
ドクン
DOKUN
WAIT THERE.

ドクン
DOKUN

AKIRA'S...
...MOVEMENTS...
...ARE SMOOTH.
IS THERE ANYTHING I CAN DO HERE?

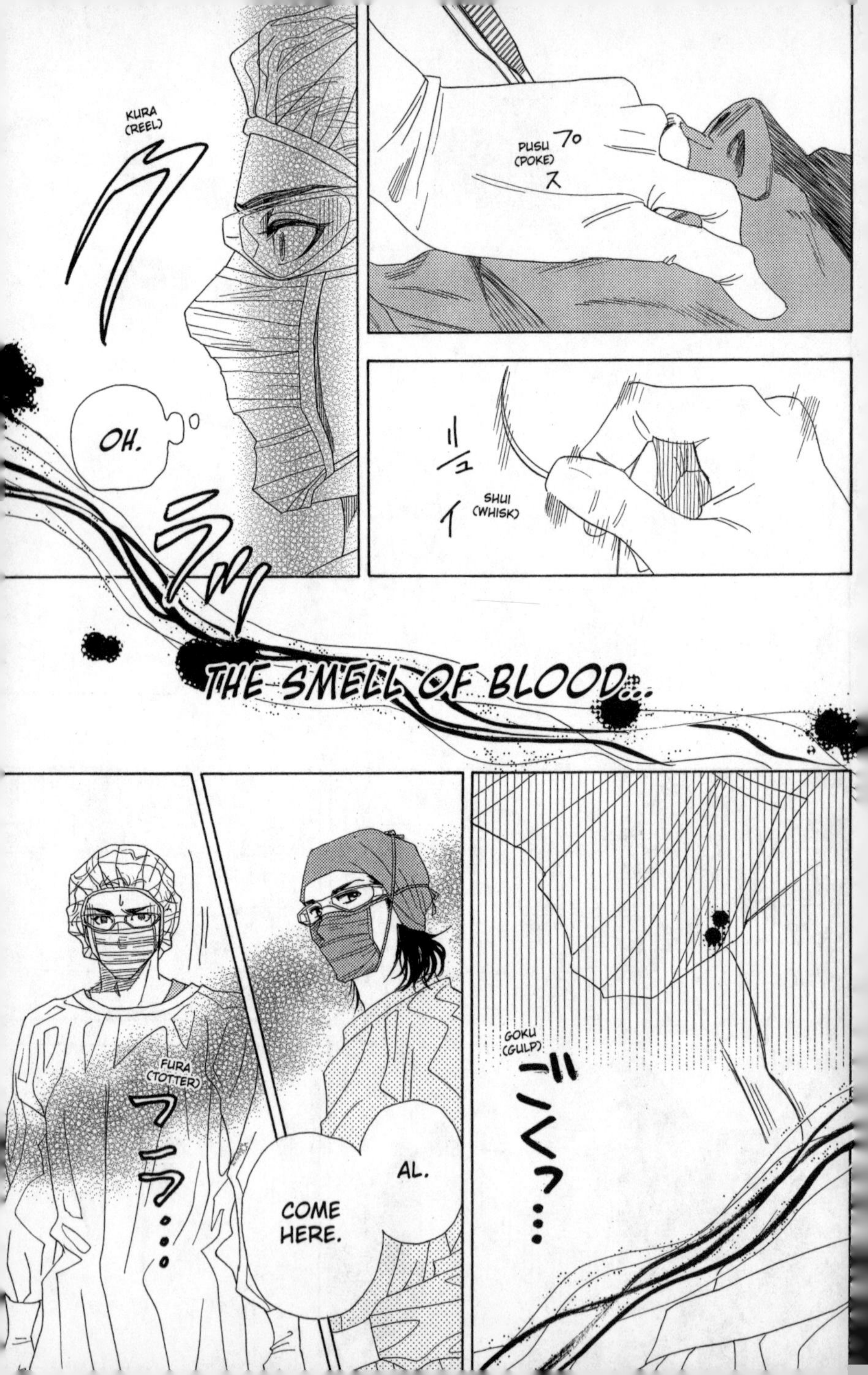
PUSU (POKE)
SHUI (WHISK)
KURA (REEL)
OH.
THE SMELL OF BLOOD...
GOKU (GULP)
AL.
COME HERE.
FURA (TOTTER)

DO YOU SERIOUSLY WANT TO HELP?
YES!
GU (CLENCH)

GU
(SQUEEZE)
グッ
HEY!
GU
グッ
DON'T BE SO ROUGH!!
YOU'LL DAMAGE HIS SKIN!!
O— OKAY.
HFF!
HFF!
THAT'S ENOUGH.
GO BACK OVER THERE.
NOT YET.
HFF!
I MASSAGE ...
...MORE.
HAH!
WHEN I NEED THAT, I'LL CALL YOU.

HFF!
HAH!
HAH!
TSU (SLIT)
DOKUN (BADMP)

DOKUN
ドクン
DOKUN
ドクン
HAH!
HAH!
DON'T YOU DARE! TOUGH IT OUT!!
DON'T LOSE TO THE SMELL OF BLOOD AND GET IN AKIRA'S WAY. THAT WOULD BE AWFUL!!
VOOON (VRRRRM)
ヴォオォーンッ
GURAA (REEL)
ぐらぁ

!?
AL!?
DAN
(WHUMP)
THIS...COULD NOT BE WORSE.
WELL, LOOK AT THAT.
ZAWA
(MURMUR)
ザワ
ZAWA
ザワ

YOU REALLY DON'T HAVE FANGS.
あ
ANGU (NOMM)
ん
ぐい
COME TO THINK OF IT...
...USUALLY WHEN HUMANS BECOME VAMPIRES, THEIR HAIR AND EYES TURN BLACK...
?
HM...
WELL, WELL.
...BUT YOUR HAIR IS LIGHT BROWN, AND YOUR EYES ARE GRAY.
...ARE THEY?
GNGH!
I USED TO HAVE LIGHT BLOND HAIR AND GREEN EYES.
AND...
...YOU SAY YOU CAN'T CONTROL YOUR TRANSFORMATION.
ザワ
ZAWA
ザワ
ZAWA
I'VE NEVER SEEN ANYONE LIKE YOU BEFORE.
LIVING UNNOTICED AMONG HUMANS ISN'T GOING TO BE EASY FOR YOU.
I SUSPECT ANY ASSOCIATION WITH THEM WILL BE DIFFICULT.

...HOW COME I'M THE ONLY ONE WHO'S NOT LIKE OTHER VAMPIRES?
EVEN AFTER SHE DRANK YOUR BLOOD, IT TOOK YOU A WHILE TO DIE, YOU SAID?
KOKU (NOD)
I'M NOT CLEAR ON THAT MYSELF, BUT...
...IT MAY BE BECAUSE SHE DIDN'T TAKE ENOUGH BLOOD.
ALSO...
...DURING THE CRUCIAL TIME WHEN YOUR CELLS WERE CHANGING...
...YOU WERE EMBALMED. THAT MIGHT HAVE CONTRIBUTED.

HA
(JOLT)
HOW ARE YOU FEELING?
I...
...FINE. H OW JOB?
I'M TAKING A BREAK.

THERE'S NO RESTORATION WORK.
THE BODY WASN'T PUT THROUGH AN AUTOPSY EITHER, SO IT WON'T EVEN TAKE TWO MORE HOURS.
YOU WERE OUT FOR ABOUT FIFTEEN MINUTES.
I SHOULD'VE EATEN MORE LIVER AT DINNER.
I'M SO LAME.
I CAME BECAUSE I WANTED TO HELP, BUT I'M JUST GETTING IN THE WAY.
HEY.
ARE YOU HUNGRY?

GIKU (FLINCH)
NOT HUNGRY.
LIAR.
WHEN I TRIED TO HELP YOU UP AFTER YOU COLLAPSED, YOU LICKED THE BLOOD OFF MY GLOVE.
IS THAT WHY YOU WANTED TO HELP ME? YOU'RE HUNGRY, AND YOU THOUGHT IF YOU PLAYED YOUR CARDS RIGHT...
...YOU'D GET THE LEFTOVER BLOOD?
NO!!

WHEN THE JOB IS DONE, I'LL GIVE YOU SOME OF MY BLOOD.
JUST LIE DOWN AND KEEP QUIET UNTIL THEN.
NO.
NO WANT BLOOD.
PIRI (KRAKL)
I WAS...
... HUNGRY, BUT...
...NO WANT YOURS.
YOUR BLOOD...
...NASTY.

BAN
(SLAM)
I LIED.
AKIRA'S BLOOD IS DELICIOUS.
IT'S TOO GOOD. IF I DRINK IT, I WON'T BE ABLE TO STOP.
I'LL KEEP GOING UNTIL HE COLLAPSES. THIS TIME, I MIGHT ACTUALLY END UP KILLING HIM.

SO...
...I'M NOT DRINKING AKIRA'S BLOOD.
カチャ
KACHA (CHAK)
COME HERE.

PRETTY.
HE LOOKS HEALTHY AND PEACEFUL...
THIS IS...
...INCREDIBLE...

REALLY...
...PRETTY.
?
AL.
OVER HERE.
IT'S MAGIC AKIRA WORKED...
......
EMBALMING YIELDS A LOT OF WASTE FLUIDS.
THIS IS ONE OF THEM.

WE STERILIZE THIS SORT OF BLOOD, THEN THROW IT AWAY...
...BUT I KEPT A LITTLE BACK.
YOU HELPED MAKE HIS BODY LOOK GOOD.
NOT MUCH, BUT YOU HELPED.
IN EXCHANGE, YOU'RE GETTING JUST A LITTLE OF WHAT WE'D THROW AWAY.
GO OVER THERE AND TELL HIM "THANK YOU" PROPERLY.
FURA (TOTTER)

—AMEN.
I'M SORRY.
I'M SORRY.
I'M SORRY.
PLEASE GRANT ME JUST A LITTLE...
...OF THE LAST OF YOUR LIFE. JUST A TINY BIT.
PLEASE... SHARE IT WITH ME.

—HIS BLOOD TASTED VERY FAINTLY...
...OF CHEMICALS.
AND, WEIRDLY...
...IT CARRIED THE FRAGRANCE OF SOUTHERN LANDS.
THANKS FOR ALL YOUR HARD WORK.
HEY.

DOES BLOOD...
...REALLY TASTE THAT DIFFERENT FROM PERSON TO PERSON?
...YEAH.
IS IT DIET? ENVIRONMENT?
OR MAYBE...MY ATTACHMENT?
AKIRA'S BLOOD IS PARTICULARLY GOOD.
YOUR BLOOD...
...NASTY.
OH, IT IS, HUH?

Around eleven P.M. yesterday, a young woman was found dead...
...by a prefectural highway near Hachi●uji after being stabbed a number of times in the back.
ACT 7 | AL WORKS HARD
TV: MURDER / WOMAN (25) / RANDOM • SAME CULPRIT
The victim is Rinka Kikuchi-san, twenty-five, an office worker.
The incident is the latest in a series of apparently random muders in the area.
TV: NEWS FLASH / ELEVEN P.M. YESTERDAY / SIMILAR METHODS • THREE VICTIMS
速報
昨夜11時
Due to the similarity of the methods, investigators suspect the same culprit is responsible for all of them.
With the discovery of the third victim, police are facing criticism for—

ACT 7 | AL WORKS HARD

FUNERAL HOME
OLD MEMORIAL CENTER
OH!
TAKATSUKA-KUN, GOOD MORNING.
GOOD MORNING.
IT SURE IS COLD AGAIN TODAY, RIGHT?
RIGHT?
GOOD MORNING, AL.
SKREE!

GOOD MORNING.
I'M AL.
ALBERT IRVING.
THAT BAT IS REALLY CLEVER, ISN'T HE?
SKREE!
SKREE!
YAY! A COMPLIMENT!
AL.
DON'T SCREECH IN MY EAR.
YOU'RE NOISY.
グッ
GU (GULP)
HE LOOKS LIKE HE KNOWS WHAT YOU SAID.
I HEAR BATS ARE GENERALLY PRETTY SMART.
カチャ
KACHA (CHAK)

TAKA-TSUKA-SAN. GOOD MORNING.
MORNING.
MORNING TO YOU TOO, AL.
KOYANAGI (28) EMBALMER
SKREE!
I LEARNED...
...FROM KOYANAGI—WHO'S ACTUALLY A NICE, CHILL DUDE DESPITE HIS TOUGH-GUY LOOKS...
...THAT AKIRA IS THIRTY.
I'M TWENTY-EIGHT, AND HE'S TWO YEARS OLDER THAN ME.
AKIRA'S THIRTY!?
ガー
GAN (SHOCK)

BASA (FLAP)
SKREE!
SKREE!
TCH!
DAMMIT.
HUH?
WHAT?
PACHIN (CLICK)
SKREE!
SKREE!
SKREE!
HUH?
WHAT?
HE SAYS IT'S NOT HIS FAVORITE NEWS PROGRAM.
PACHI
UH...
HUH...

AL REALLY IS CUTE, ISN'T HE?
HOW DID YOU TAME HIM?
I JUST SORT OF DID.
YOU CAN DOMESTICATE THEM LIKE THIS BY ACCIDENT?
ピルルル
PIRURU (RRRING)
HELLO?
...REALLY DOESN'T COMMUNICATE WITH PEOPLE.
WHEN I STARTED COMING TO WORK WITH HIM, I REALIZED SOMETHING.
AKIRA...
I-DIDN'T THINK HE WAS SUCH A QUIET GUY.
WHEN HE'S WITH ME, HE'S ALWAYS ANGRY AND NAGGING.

KACHI (CLICK)
カチ
WHAT WAS THAT ABOUT?
A CLIENT'S MAKEUP ISN'T HOLDING WELL, AND THEY'RE CONCERNED ABOUT IT.
I'M GOING TO THE FUNERAL.
OH...THE ONE FROM YESTERDAY.
I THINK I'LL STAY AND ATTEND THE CEREMONY.
ALL RIGHT.
FUNERAL...
バタン
BATAN (SHUT)
DOES THAT MEAN HE'S GOING TO CHANGE INTO A SUIT?
WHEN AKIRA'S DRESSED UP AND LOOKING SHARP, HE'S SO HANDSOME, YOU CAN'T HELP BUT STARE!
KREE!
SKREE!
ビクッ
BIKU (FLINCH)
HUH!?
WHAT!?

GOOOOD MORNING!
BAN (BAM)
OH!
AL! ♡
GOOD MORNING!
SKREE! SKREE! SKREE! KREE!
GURI
GURI (SKWOOSH)
HE'S SOOO KEWT! ♡
IF THEY ALL GET THIS AFFECTIONATE, I WANT A BAT OF MY OWN.
MARUYAMA (22) ASSOCIATE EMBALMER KOYANAGI'S ASSISTANT
THAT BAT'S A SPECIAL CASE.
IT WOULDN'T BE THAT EASY.
...OR THAT'S WHAT TAKATSUKA-SAN SAID.
SO.
BOSO (MUTTER)
TSUNO (22) ASSOCIATE EMBALMER AKIRA'S ASSISTANT

SPECIAL, HUH...?
AL REALLY IS STARTLINGLY CLEVER.
EVEN WHEN HE'S LOOSE LIKE THIS, HE BEHAVES HIMSELF, AND HE DOESN'T MAKE A MESS ANYWHERE.
I WAS PRETTY SURPRISED WHEN TAKATSUKA-SAN FIRST BROUGHT HIM IN—WEREN'T YOU?
YEAH.
IT WAS LIKE, "*THAT* TAKATSUKA-SAN!? REALLY!?"
ON TOP OF THAT, HE SAID IT WAS BECAUSE, "IF I LEAVE HIM ALONE IN MY APARTMENT, HE GETS EMOTIONALLY UNSTABLE"...
OH! I GET THAT, THOUGH. AL'S A TOTAL PEOPLE-BAT.
UNLIKE HIS OWNER, HE'S FRIENDLY.
DON'T YOU THINK TAKATSUKA-SAN'S GOTTEN MORE APPROACHABLE SINCE AL STARTED COMING?
HE'S BECOME A REAL IDOL AROUND HERE.
IDOL!?
YEAH, HE HAS.
HAS HE?
......

PAN (SMACK)
SPEAKING OF THAT...
THE PART-TIMER WHO'S BEEN CLEANING THE PREP ROOM AND THE CDC ROOM* IS A FOREIGNER.
DID YOU KNOW?
*THE ROOM WHERE COSMETICS ARE APPLIED AND THE BODY IS DRESSED BEFORE BEING PLACED IN A COFFIN.
I CAUGHT A GLIMPSE OF HIM ONCE, BUT I DIDN'T SEE HIS FACE.
I'M NEVER HERE THAT LATE...
PIKU (PERK)
PART-TIMER?
SO THAT GUY?
HE'S EXTREMELY HOT.
I WAS LIKE, "WHAT IS A MODEL DOING HERE!?"
OH-HO. IS THAT RIGHT?
ARE THEY TALKING ABOUT ME?
YEAH.

RECENTLY, I LANDED A PART-TIME JOB.
I START AT SIX P.M., AFTER I REVERT FROM BAT TO HUMAN, SO IT'S ONLY A COUPLE HOURS A DAY.
I'M STILL HAPPY ABOUT IT, THOUGH.
WHEN AKIRA COMES IN FOR RUSH JOBS, I HELP HIM, AND HE LETS ME HAVE SOME OF THE BLOOD.
I'M A JANITOR FOR THE EMBALMING FACILITY...
SHAKIIIN (SHING)
AL AS A HUMAN.
OH, ALSO! WHEN I'M WORKING, I GO BY "CAIN BATZ."
GI (CREAK)
I'VE NEVER SEEN THE PART-TIMER, BUT I HEAR...
...TAKATSUKA-SAN'S THE ONE WHO REFERRED HIM.
...HERE AT OLD MEMORIAL CENTER.

HUH!? DID HE REALLY?
ACCORDING TO MATSUMURA-SAN, HE'S AN ASPIRING EMBALMER.
IT DOES SEEM ODD THAT HE CAME HERE INSTEAD OF STUDYING IN AMERICA WHERE THIS STUFF IS MAINSTREAM, BUT WHATEVER.
BY THE WAY... IT'S PAST STARTING TIME. WHERE'S TAKATSUKA-SAN?
HE MUST BE HERE IF AL IS.
HE'S AT A FUNERAL. HE HAD TO GO FIX THE MAKEUP ON A CLIENT.
HE SAID HE'S STAYING FOR THE CEREMONY.
HUH!?
BUT... I'M HIS ASSISTANT. HE DIDN'T CALL ME.
OH, UH... YOU KNOW. HE'S IMPATIENT. HE'S NOT GOOD AT WAITING.
......
RIGHT...

BASASA (FLUTTER)
!!
IT'S JAPANESE. LOOKS HARD.
WASHA (SCRITCH)
SKREE!
SKREE!
SENSEI? QUESTION.
HM? LET'S SEE.

OH.
IN THIS CASE, FOR EXAMPLE...
HAAH...
TSUNO?
SIGHING?
ちょい ちょい
CHOI (TWEAK)
CHOI
AAAAAAH...
YOUR OWNER...
...SURE HATES ME, DOESN'T HE?
HATE?
AKIRA HATES TSUNO...?
IS THAT WHAT HE THINKS?

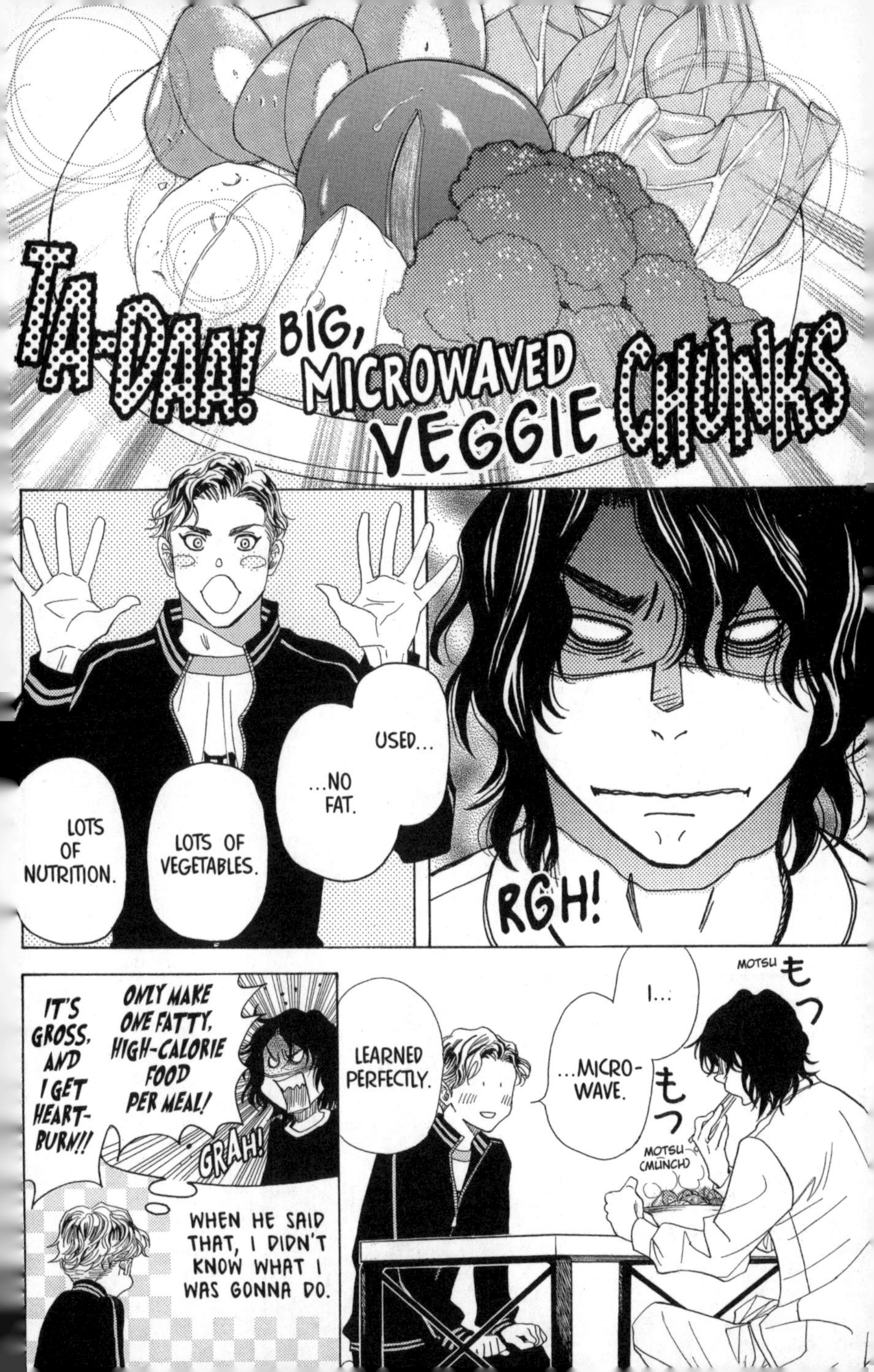
TA-DAA! BIG, MICROWAVED VEGGIE CHUNKS
RGH!
USED...
...NO FAT.
LOTS OF VEGETABLES.
LOTS OF NUTRITION.
MOTSU もっ もっ MOTSU (MUNCH)
I...
...MICRO-WAVE.
LEARNED PERFECTLY.
ONLY MAKE ONE FATTY, HIGH-CALORIE FOOD PER MEAL!
IT'S GROSS, AND I GET HEART-BURN!!
GRAH!
WHEN HE SAID THAT, I DIDN'T KNOW WHAT I WAS GONNA DO.

JI (STARE)
じっ
WHAT?
IT... IT GOOD?
IT JUST TASTES LIKE VEGETABLES.
I WONDER...
HAS AKIRA EVER COOKED FOR SOMEBODY...
...OR HAD SOMEBODY COOK FOR HIM LIKE THIS BEFORE?
A—
AKIRA.

YOU HATE...
...TSUNO?
TSUNO?
YOU MEAN MY ASSISTANT?
KOKU (NOD)
WHY WOULD YOU ASK ME THAT?
TSUNO...
...THINK YOU HATE...
...HIM.
I HATE HIM?
WHO SAID THAT?
HYOI (HOP)
ひょい
TSUNO.

DOSA (FWUMP)
ドサッ
MUSU (SULK)
むすっ
YOU NOT TAKE HIM TO JOB.
EMERGENCY.
HE NOT ABLE HELP YOU.
THAT GUY...
I THOUGHT HE'D SEEMED PRICKLY LATELY. SO HE'S BEEN THINKING DUMB STUFF LIKE THAT, HUH?
AKIRA!
YOU NOT TALK WITH TSUNO.
THAT NOT OKAY !!
GAN (WHAM)

IT'S WORK!!
IT'S NOT AS IF WE'RE FRIENDS. WHY SHOULD I TALK TO HIM MORE THAN I NEED TO!?
THAT...
...WRONG.
TALKING IMPORTANT.
YOU NOT KNOW FEELINGS!!
GRR!
PINPOOON (DING-DONG)
TCH!
YOU GET THAT.
AKIRA.

PINPOOON
ピーホーーン
I NOT APOLOGIZE.
I NOT WRONG.
BUT...
ピーホーーン
PINPOOON
...DON'T HATE ME. OKAY?

ガチャ
GACHA (KACHAK)
OH!
NUKA-RIYA...
THAT RANDOM KILLING THREE DAYS AGO...
DID YOU HEAR ABOUT IT?
YEAH. SAW ON TV.
TAKE A LOOK AT THIS.
THEY DON'T LOOK LIKE THE SKETCH, BUT...
...THESE THREE ARE CONSIDERED SUSPECTS RIGHT NOW.
IS HE IN THERE?
じー
JI (STARE)

NO.
DAM-MIT!
WE STRUCK OUT, HUH!?
GUSHA (SHUFF)
ぐしゃっ
SO WE KNOW THEY'RE DEAD ENDS, AND WE STILL HAVE TO GO GET THEIR ALIBIS.
THIS IS A DISASTER.
くんっ
KUN (SNIFF)
NUKA-RIYA.
WOMAN'S PERFUME.
I SMELL...
...A LITTLE.
?
GIRL-FRIEND?
OH. NOW THAT YOU MENTION IT...
I WAS WEARING THIS COAT AT THE CRIME SCENE.
THE VICTIM COLLECTED FRAGRANCES, BUT...
...THAT WAS THREE DAYS AGO.

MY NOSE GOOD.
MY BAT NOSE...
...MORE GOOD.
COULD YOU MAYBE...
...FOLLOW A TRAIL OF OLD BLOOD?
LIKE A POLICE DOG?
NEVER DONE IT.
DUNNO.
COULD YOU TRY IT?
THERE ARE NO WITNESSES AND NOTHING LEFT BEHIND. WE'RE STUCK.
WHILE WE'RE BOGGED DOWN INVESTIGATING, HE MAY STRIKE AGAIN.
IF IT GIVES US A SHOT AT FINDING THE KILLER, I'LL TRY ANYTHING!!

DID THAT GUY...
...DO TO A GIRL WHO SMELLED THIS NICE...
...WHAT HE DID TO ME?
DID HE SMILE...
...AS HE STABBED HER?
WHILE HE KILLED HER?
NUKA-RIYA.

I WILL TRY.
I ALSO WANT KNOW...
...IF I CAN DO IT.
MAGAZINE: HOME APPLIANCE REVIEW
FOLLOW A TRAIL OF BLOOD...
...HM?
YEAH.
NOT SURE I CAN DO IT.
MAYBE YOU CAN, MAYBE NOT...
...BUT EVEN IF YOU CAN'T TRACK HIM, YOU'RE NOT RESPONSIBLE.
SIM

I BET NUKARIYA ...
...IS GRASPING AT STRAWS.
GRASP?
STRAWS?
IF THERE'S EVEN A LITTLE HOPE, EVEN IF HE KNOWS IT'S POINTLESS...
...HE'LL TRY IT ANYWAY.
MM-HMM. I SEE.
WELL, EITHER WAY.
GUSHA (MUSS)
ぐしゃ
GO DO YOUR BEST DOG IMPRESSION.
GUSHA
ぐしゃ
GUSHA
ぐしゃ
GRRR!
DOG !?
......
NO...

HE'S ACTUALLY...
AKIRA.
YOU NOT...
...MAD NOW?
...NO.
I'VE ALREADY FORGOTTEN ABOUT IT.
...TRYING TO MAKE ME FEEL BETTER.

英会話
Neva
駅前留学
○井歯科
コンタクトのミタ
COCO
チラ
CHIRA (GLANCE)
SIGN: ENGLISH CONVERSATION / NEVA / STUDY ABROAD AT HOME
ERM...
NUKA-RIYA-SAN.
...A BAT... ISN'T IT.
YES, IT IS.
THAT'S, UM...

WE'RE ON OUR WAY TO A CRIME SCENE.
WHAT ARE YOU GOING TO DO WITH IT?
I HEARD THEY HAVE EXCELLENT NOSES, SO I BORROWED HIM FROM A FRIEND.
I THOUGHT I'D HAVE HIM FOLLOW THE BLOOD TRAIL.
I'VE NEVER HEARD OF BATS BEING USED IN AN INVESTIGATION.
YOU'RE SURE YOU DON'T NEED TO GET PERMISSION?
BESIDES, THAT'S NOT THE JOB WE WERE ASSIGNED...
DETECTIVE YANAGAWA.
AS LONG AS YOU KEEP QUIET, THERE WON'T BE ANY TROUBLE.
HUH?
B-BUT...THIS DOESN'T SEEM LIKE A GREAT IDEA.
IF YOU DON'T LIKE THE WAY I WORK...
...YOU CAN GO HOME.

......
IT'S NOT...
MMBL...
...ABOUT WHETHER I LIKE IT OR NOT...
MMBL...
ジッ
JI (STARE)
NUKARIYA'S KIND OF...
HE'S GENERALLY NICE, BUT...
...IS HE ACTUALLY PRETTY STRICT?
ニコ
NIKO (SMILE)
ニコ
NIKO
ドキ
DOKI (BADMP)
ドキ
DOKI

BATAN (SLAM)
PI (BEEP)
SIGN: ROYAL CLINIC
AL.
IT'S BEEN HOSED DOWN. CAN YOU SMELL IT ANYWAY?
THIS IS IT!! THIS PLACE REEKS OF BLOOD!!
KOKURI (NOD)
BA (FLAP)

HFF!
FOR THE LOVE OF—!
WEEZ!
HFF!
HOW FAR IS IT GOING!?
HFF!
AL.
HELP US OUT.
OH...
THE SMELL'S GETTING FAINTER.
FUWA (DRIFT)
ation
DID HE RIDE A BIKE FROM HERE?

HYUN (WHIZZ)
EEK!
I CAN SMELL ANOTHER KIND OF BLOOD NOW, MIXED WITH THE FIRST ONE.
WHAT IS THIS?
WHY ARE THE BLOOD-SCENTS OVERLAPPING LIKE THIS?
SIGN: BUS STOP / CENTRAL BUS / ELEMENTARY SCHOOL ENTRANCE
KUN (SNIFF)
くん
KUN
くん
バスのりば
Bus stop
中央バス
小学校入口
BA (FLAP)
KUN (SNIFF)
BUWA (SHUDDER)

A THIRD SCENT.
THAT'S MY BLOOD!!
AL!
SKREE!
BUN (SHAKE)
ぶん
BUN
ぶん
DID YOU LOSE THE TRAIL?
THAT'S NOT IT?
TIME FOR A BREAK, THEN?
WE'VE GOT A BIG YOUNG GUY WITH NO STAMINA HERE.
GRRNH!
HFF!
I WANT TO TELL HIM THE KILLER LIVES NEARBY, BUT I CAN'T!

HFF!
WEEZ!
HFF!
HAH!
WEEZ!
A... A BAT ISN'T... GOING TO...
...BE ANY...
HFF!
YOU'VE GOT ENOUGH ENERGY LEFT TO TALK?
BA (FLAP)
AH.
COME ON!
YEEE!
A FOURTH KIND OF BLOOD.
THIS IS NUTS.
THERE ARE FOUR DIFFERENT BLOOD-SCENTS MIXED TOGETHER.
THIS IS...

THIS IS...!!
HERE!
SKREE!
AL!!
SKREE!

WEEZ!
THE BAT SAYS THIS IS THE PLACE?
HFF!
HFF!
THIS IS SHIBAZAKI-SAN'S TEAM'S AREA, ISN'T IT?
SKREE!
IF THEY FIND OUT WE WENT IN WITHOUT PERMIS-SION...
...WON'T THERE BE TROUBLE?
THERE PROBABLY WILL BE.
BUT...
...WE'LL CATCH THE PERP.
WHICH WOULD YOU PREFER? HAVING ANOTHER VICTIM TURN UP BECAUSE WE TRIED TO SAVE FACE?
OR GETTING TO ARREST THE KILLER, NO MATTER WHAT IT DOES TO US?
WELL...
MMBL...
GETTING TO ARREST HIM WOULD BE...
MMBL...
I'M GLAD YOU'VE GOT COMMON SENSE.

THE KILLER IS IN THIS BUILDING.
THERE'S NO DOUBT ABOUT IT.
ピ
PI (BEEP)
とじる
ひらく
ピ
PI
ピ
PI
BUTTONS: OPEN, CLOSE
ERM...
WHY DID YOU PUSH ALL THE FLOORS?
ポーン
POOON (DIIING)
SNIFF
SNIFF
......
FURU FURU (SHAKE)
ふる ふる
ガー
GAAA (VRRRR)

POOON
ポーン
PON (DING)
ポン
PON
ポン
SNIFF
SNIFF
BA (FOOM)
バッ
HERE!!
AH!
CAN'T IT JUST—
AGH!
BASASA (FLUTTER)
バサッ
TA (TMP)
たっ

SKREE!
SO THIS IS THE PLACE.
SKREE!
RGH...
BIIII (BZZZZ)
BIIII
DON'T SAY A WORD.

...YES?
WHO IS IT?
ブルッ
BURU (SHUDDER)
THAT VOICE!!
IT'S THE ONE FROM THE PARK!!
EXCUSE ME. WE'RE WITH THE POLICE.
THE POLICE?
THEY CAME BY ALREADY, TWO DAYS AGO.
I'M SORRY TO DISTURB YOU AGAIN.
WE'RE SPEAKING TO EVERYONE IN THE AREA ONE MORE TIME.
ガチャ
GACHA (KACHAK)
もわっ
MOWA (WAFT)

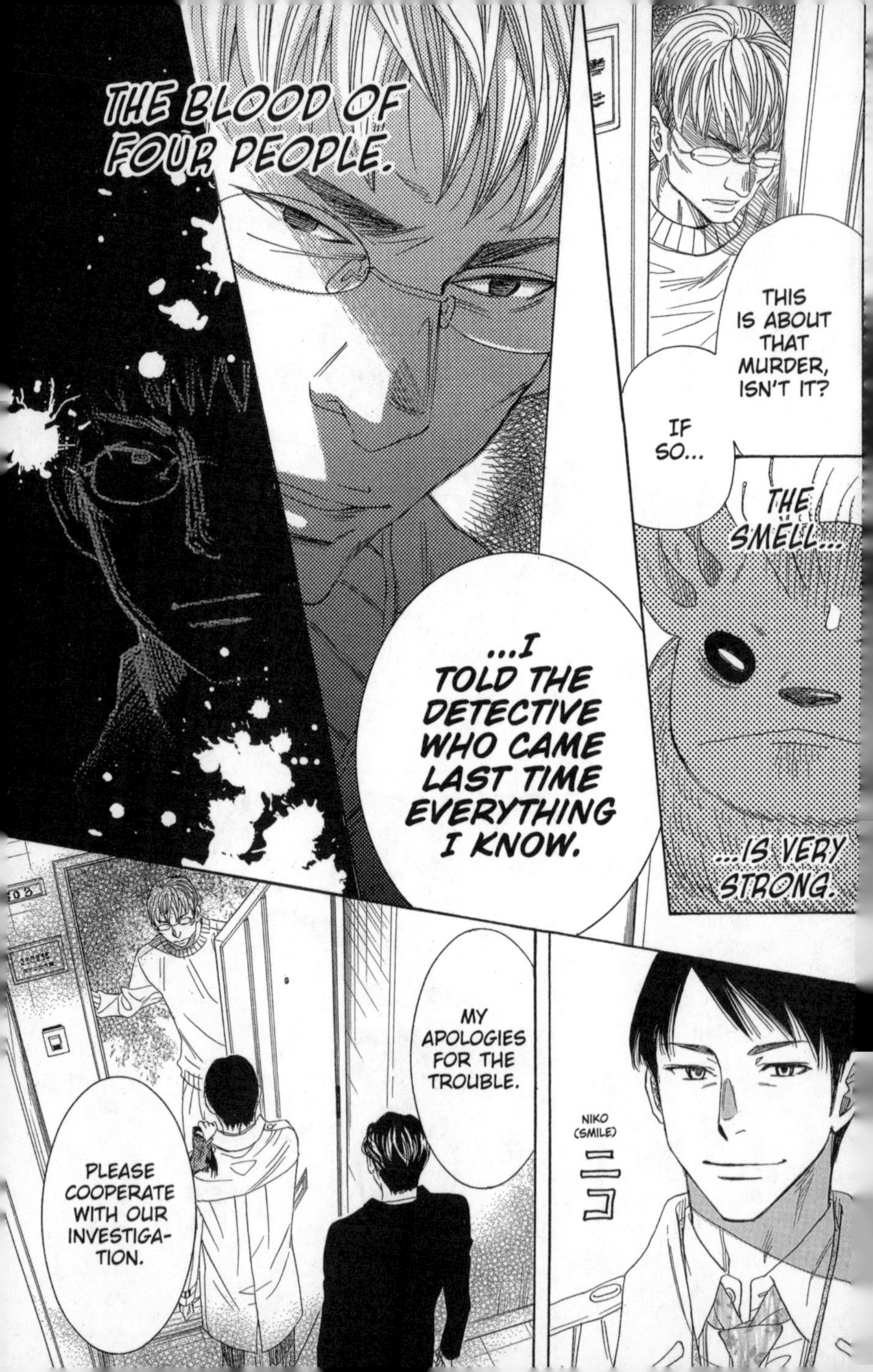
THIS IS ABOUT THAT MURDER, ISN'T IT?
IF SO...
...I TOLD THE DETECTIVE WHO CAME LAST TIME EVERYTHING I KNOW.
THE SMELL...
...IS VERY STRONG.
THE BLOOD OF FOUR PEOPLE.
NIKO (SMILE)
MY APOLOGIES FOR THE TROUBLE.
PLEASE COOPERATE WITH OUR INVESTIGA-TION.

DAN (WHAM)
WHAT EXACTLY ...
...WAS THAT?
WE FOUND THE PLACE, AND THEN...
...ALL YOU DID WAS TALK ABOUT INNOCUOUS STUFF, AND NOW WE'RE LEAVING!?
EXPLAIN YOURSELF! YOU'RE NOT SERIOUSLY GOING TO TELL ME...
...THAT GUY WAS THE PERP, ARE YOU!?
THAT'S RIGHT.
HE'S THE KILLER.
...HUH?
THAT'S RIDICULOUS.
I MEAN, THERE'S NO PROOF.
POOON (DIIING)
THE BAT FOLLOWED THE SCENT HERE, DIDN'T HE?

IT'S JUST A BAT.
HOW AM I SUPPOSED TO BELIEVE THAT?
"JUST"?
SU (SHF)
...HUH?
WHAT'S ...?
A COMPOSITE SKETCH OF THE PERP.
YOU MEAN THERE WAS A WITNESS!?
WHY HAVEN'T YOU TOLD THE HIGHER-UPS!?
HIS SITUATION IS COMPLICATED, AND I CAN'T GET HIM INVOLVED WITH THE POLICE.
B-BUT...
THIS IS REALLY IMPORTANT.

I JUST TOLD YOU...
...I *CAN'T GET HIM INVOLVED.*
THE WITNESS IS AN ILLEGAL ALIEN.
HE'S A VICTIM AS WELL, BUT DUE TO HIS SITUATION, HE CAN'T REPORT IT TO THE POLICE.
NO ONE KNOWS WHO HE IS.
THERE'S NO PROOF HE SAW THIS GUY. NO PROOF HE WAS STABBED.
WHO'D BELIEVE A STORY LIKE THAT?
GRR!
LISTEN UP.
ONCE WE'RE OUTSIDE, DON'T TURN AROUND.
HE'S DEFINITELY GOING TO BE WATCHING.
TON (THMP)
DON'T DO ANYTHING THAT MIGHT MAKE HIM THINK WE SUSPECT.
WE'RE GOING BACK TO THE STATION.
WE'LL CONTACT THE BUILDING MANAGER...
...AND CHECK INTO THAT GUY'S BACK-GROUND.
I WANT YOU TO REVIEW NEARBY SECURITY CAMERA FOOTAGE FROM THE DAYS OF PREVIOUS INCIDENTS.

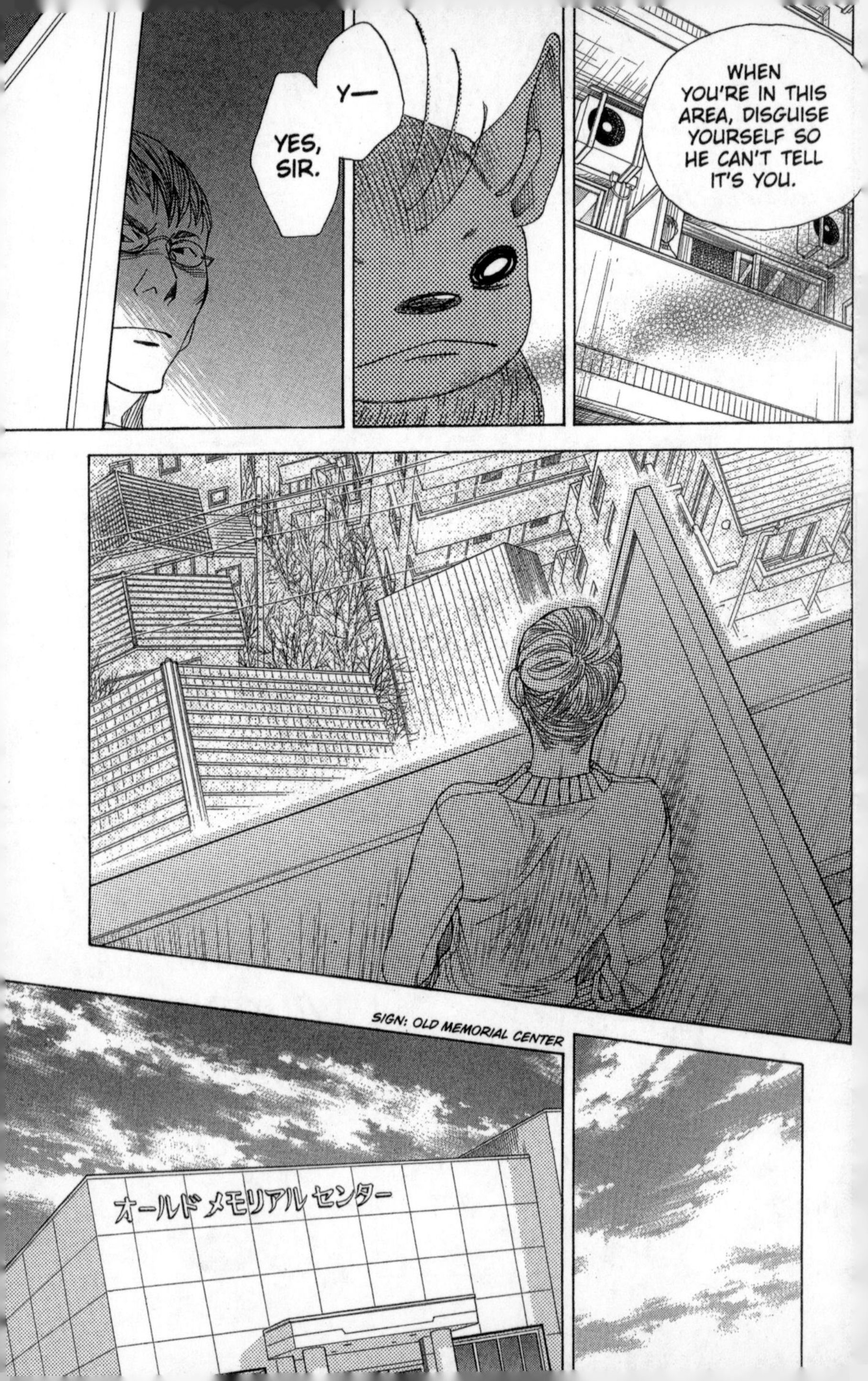
WHEN YOU'RE IN THIS AREA, DISGUISE YOURSELF SO HE CAN'T TELL IT'S YOU.
Y—
YES, SIR.
SIGN: OLD MEMORIAL CENTER
オールド メモリアル センター

DOKI (BADMP)
DOKI
I FOUND THE KILLER!!
I WAS USEFUL!!
AAAAAAAH!! WHY ISN'T IT EVENING YET!?
BASA (FLAP)
BASA
I WANT TO TELL AKIRA!
AAAARGH!! HURRY UP!! HURRY UUUUUP!!
KACHA (KACHAK)
HUH?

WHAT...
...IS AL...
...DOING...
...HERE?
BABYUN (WHIZZZ)
ビュー
RGH.
SKREE!
SKREE!
SKREE!
SHUT UP.
BE QUIET ALREADY.
SKREE!
SKREE!
SKREE!
SKREE!
I SAID...
...PIPE DOWN!!
SHUN (DROOP)
しゅん…
GEEZ.

AL...
...WASN'T HERE THIS MORNING.
I'M CURIOUS...
...BUT IF I JUST ASK "WHAT HAPPENED?" HE'LL...
DON (WHAM)
...HUH?
UM... WHAT'S THIS?
THE LATEST INDUSTRY INFO FROM AMERICA.
YOU CAN READ ENGLISH, CAN'T YOU?
Y-YES, SORT OF.
IF YOU WORK BY THE BOOK, EVEN IF YOU DO THIS FOR YEARS, THAT'S AS FAR AS YOU'LL GO.

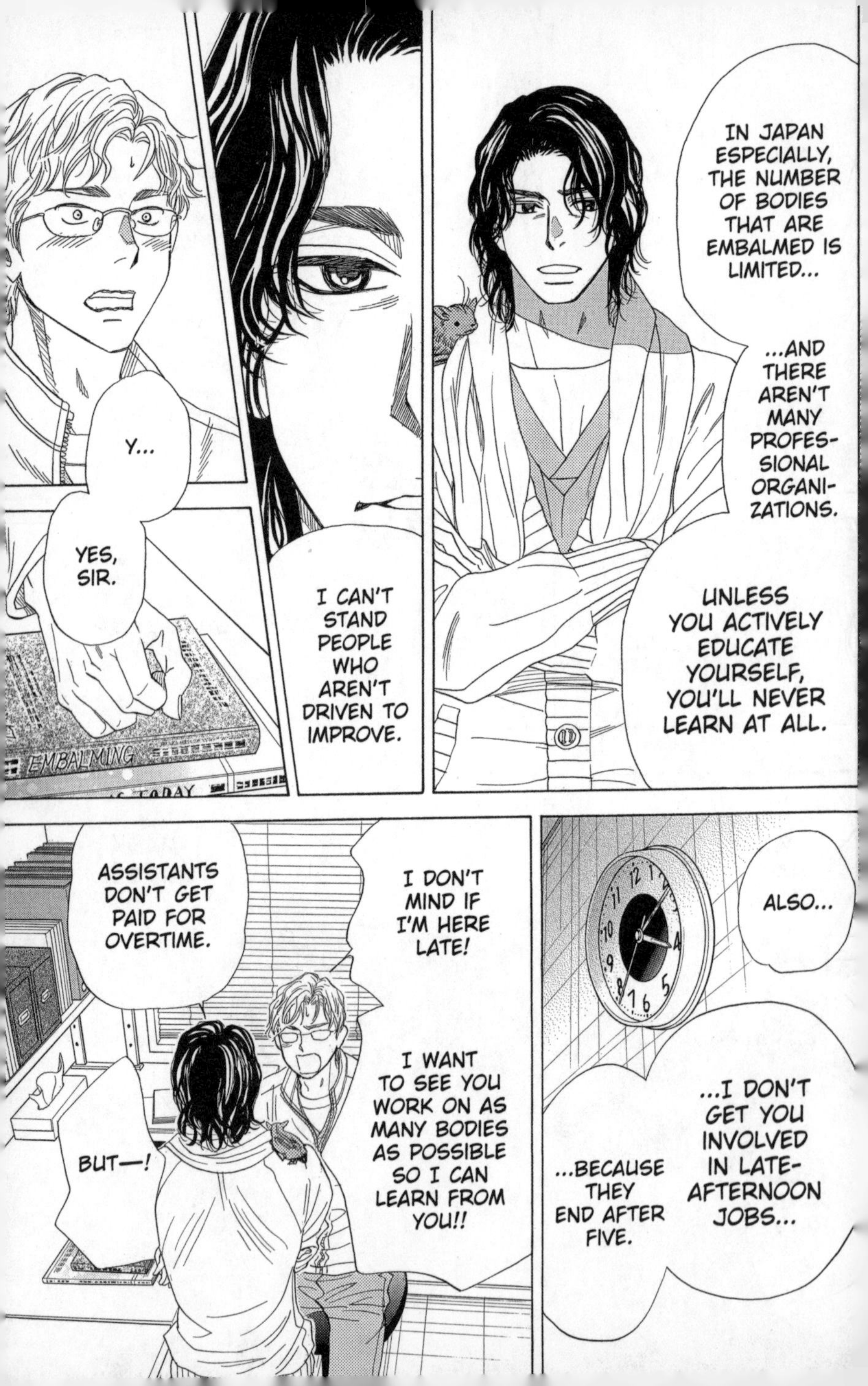

IN JAPAN ESPECIALLY, THE NUMBER OF BODIES THAT ARE EMBALMED IS LIMITED...
...AND THERE AREN'T MANY PROFES-SIONAL ORGANI-ZATIONS.
UNLESS YOU ACTIVELY EDUCATE YOURSELF, YOU'LL NEVER LEARN AT ALL.
I CAN'T STAND PEOPLE WHO AREN'T DRIVEN TO IMPROVE.
Y...
YES, SIR.
EMBALMING
ALSO...
...I DON'T GET YOU INVOLVED IN LATE-AFTERNOON JOBS...
...BECAUSE THEY END AFTER FIVE.
ASSISTANTS DON'T GET PAID FOR OVERTIME.
BUT—!
I DON'T MIND IF I'M HERE LATE!
I WANT TO SEE YOU WORK ON AS MANY BODIES AS POSSIBLE SO I CAN LEARN FROM YOU!!

NO MATTER HOW MANY JOBS YOU WATCH, YOU WON'T LEARN MUCH IF YOUR KNOWLEDGE IS INCOMPLETE.
DON'T YOU THINK ASSISTANTS ARE ONLY SUPPOSED TO WORK UNTIL FIVE...
...BECAUSE THEY WANT YOU TO STUDY AFTER THAT?
THAT'S HOW I SEE IT.
YOU'RE ONLY AN ASSISTANT FOR A YEAR.
STUDY HARD.
...I WILL.
THANK YOU, SIR.
ARE YOU HAPPY NOW...
...YOU DAMN BAT?

SKREE?
?
SKREE?
?
......
きゅーーーん
KYUUUUN (SWOOON)

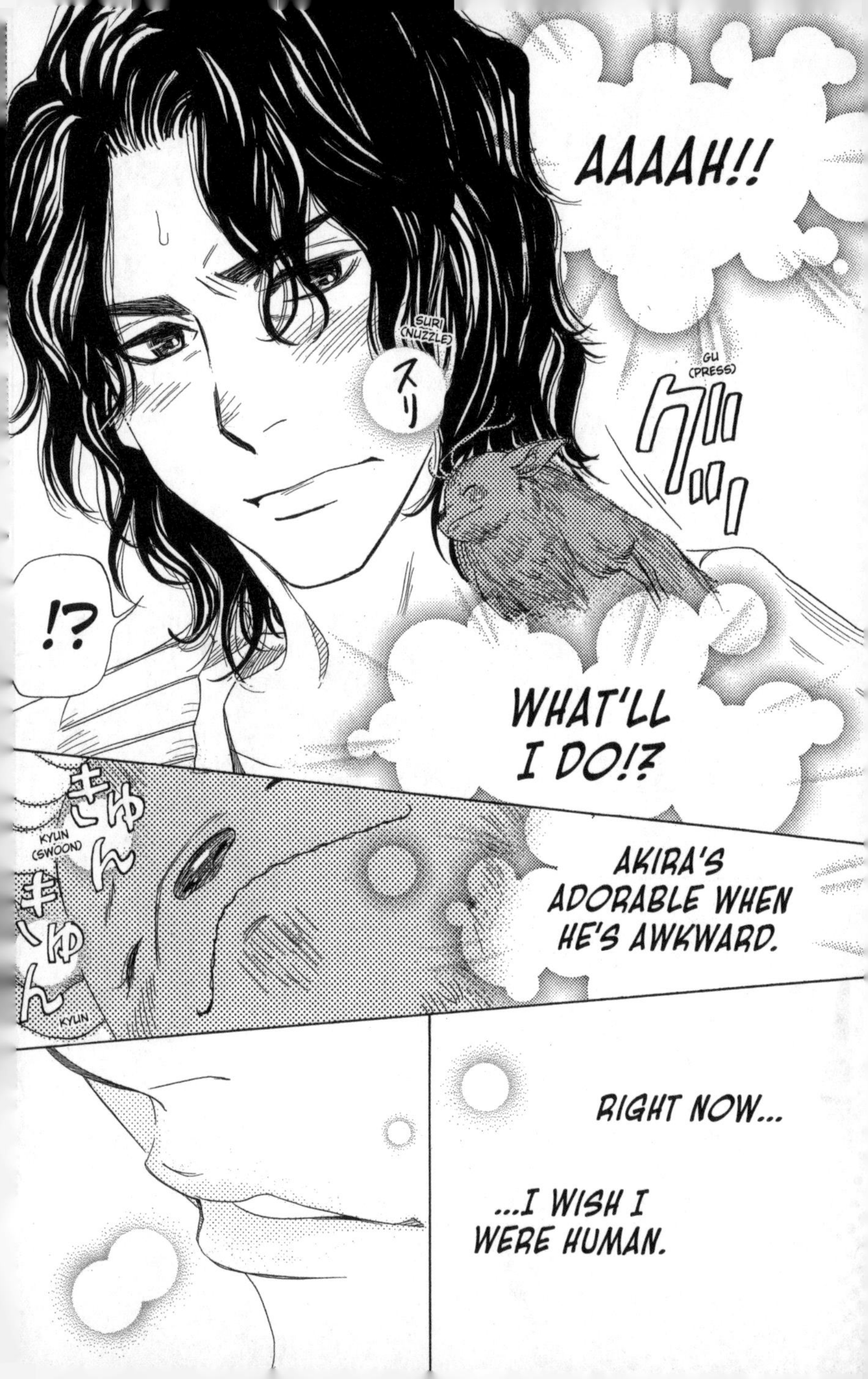
AAAAH!!
GU (PRESS)
グッ
SURI (NUZZLE)
スリ
!?
WHAT'LL I DO!?
AKIRA'S ADORABLE WHEN HE'S AWKWARD.
きゅんきゅん
KYUN (SWOON)
KYUN
RIGHT NOW...
...I WISH I WERE HUMAN.

I'D HOLD HIM CLOSE...
...AND KISS HIM...
12 December
ABOUT THAT KILLER...

NUKARIYA SENT ME A TEXT SAYING THERE'S NO PROOF...
...SO THEY CAN'T ARREST HIM.
PROOF?
PROOF THAT HE'S THE ONE WHO DID THE KILLING.
YOU CAN'T POSSIBLY EXPECT THEM TO SAY A BAT FOLLOWED THE SCENT OF BLOOD TO THE GUY.
HIS ALIBI'S PERFECT...
...AND HIS PRIVATE LIFE IS CLEAN. THEY CAN'T FIND ANY OPENINGS TO EXPLOIT.
HE IS KILLER.
NOT MISTAKE.
HE STABBED ME!
NOBODY'S DOUBTING YOU.
NUKARIYA HAS IT WORSE. HE KNOWS THE GUY'S GUILTY...
...AND YET, HE CAN'T GET HIM.
RRGH...

AFTER I FOUND HIM AND EVERYTHING!! IT'S NOT FAIR!!
ARRRGH!!
WHAT ARE WE GONNA DO IF HE GETS AWAY WHILE WE'RE FUMBLING AROUND!?
WE HAVE TO FIND SOLID PROOF...!!
TAKA-TSUKA-SAN?
DID AL STAY HOME TODAY?
THERE WAS SOMEPLACE HE WANTED TO GO.
"HE WANTED TO"...?
HE SAYS HE'LL BE BACK AT THE ENTRANCE THIS EVENING.
"HE'LL... BE BACK"...?
......

THAT SMELL.
WHEN HE OPENED THE DOOR...
...THE SMELL OF BLOOD ALMOST CHOKED ME.
IT REMINDED ME OF THE SLAUGHTERS AT JAN'S FACTORY.
THE KILLER MUST HAVE SOMETHING BLOODY STORED IN HIS ROOM.
!!

THAT'S, UH... THAT YANAGAWA GUY.
IS THE 'STACHE A DISGUISE?
FUWA (FLIT)
フワ
SKREE!
YAGH!
HUH?
HUH!?
IS THIS THE BAT FROM EARLIER?
BASASA (FLAPPA)
バサッ
SKREE!
YES, IT IS!
AGH!
STAY BACK!
GOD, THAT'S CREEPY!
I HATE ANIMALS!!
SKREE!
GOOD WORK, GUY!
GRR!
HMPH.
NOW I GET WHY NUKARIYA WAS SO RUDE TO HIM.

WELL, IF YANAGAWA'S WATCHING THIS PLACE...
...THAT MEANS THE GUY'S HOME RIGHT NOW.
LAST TIME...
...HE WAS LOOKING DOWN FROM HERE.
BASASA (FLUTTER)
KREE!
SKREEE!
SKREEE!
HM?
THAT BAT...
SKREEE, SKREEE!
WHAT'S IT DOING?

SKREEE!
KREE!
SKREE!
SKREE!
カチ
KACHI (CLICK)
NOW!!
バサッ
BASA (FLAP)

SUI (SWISH)
スイッ
BUWA (SHUDDER)
ぶわっ
FOUR DIFFERENT BLOOD-SCENTS, ALL MIXED TOGETHER!!
TA (TUP)
タッ

SNIFF
SNIFF
WHERE IS IT?
WHERE'S HE HIDING THE PROOF!?
THE SMELL IS STRONGEST...
...NEAR THE CLOSET, AND...
...THE DESK DRAWER.
PISHAN (SLIDE)
ピシャーンッ
!?
OH.

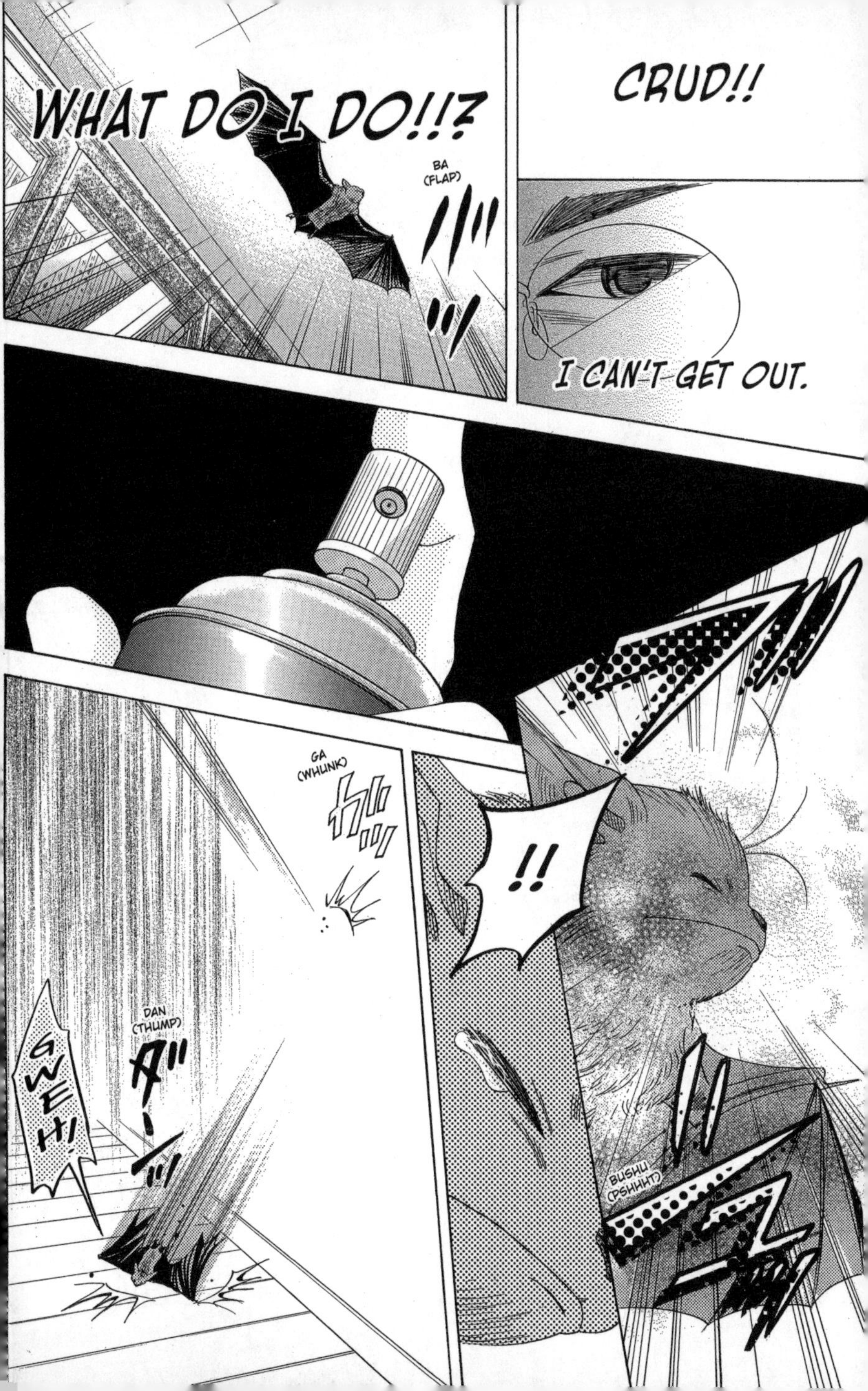
CRUD!!
I CAN'T GET OUT.
WHAT DO I DO!!?
BA (FLAP)
BUSHU (PSHHHT)
!!
GA (WHUNK)
DAN (THUMP)
GWEH!

KREE!
IT HURTS!
バタ
BATA (FLAIL)
バタ
BATA
GUKREE...
MY LUNGS—
BAN (WHAM)
SKRK...
DAMN BAT.
PREPARE TO RECEIVE DIVINE PUNISHMENT.
WHEW.

ACT 8 | In a Land on the Far Edge of Asia

AKIRA.
AKIRA.
LISTEN.
I FOUND THE KILLER.
MY NOSE WAS USEFUL TO SOMEBODY.

JYAKIN (SNICK)
FOR YOU...
...THAT WAS PRETTY GOOD WORK.

KREE!
JYAKI (SNIP)
JYAKI
OW!!
SKREEEE!
OH.
YOU AREN'T DEAD?
IT HURTS!!

バサ
BASA (FLAP)
WHOA!
バサ
BASA
ガッ
GA (KICK)
ズリ
ZURI (DRAG)
ズリ
ZURI
HUH.
ガッ
GA (GRAB)
SKREE! SKREE! KREE!
I GUESS YOU REALLY CAN'T FLY WITH YOUR WINGS CLIPPED.

BIRON (TUG)
びろんっ
SAY...
...ARE YOU THE BAT THAT DETECTIVE HAD ON HIS SHOULDER?
GU (SQUEEZE)
PAKYA (SNAP)
SU (SHF)
SOME-WHERE...
GATA (SHAKE)
GATA

...YOU MUST HAVE A TRANSMITTER OR A MICROPHONE...
...RIGGED UP INSIDE...
...I'LL BET.
ZAKU (SKASH)

ARGH...
DAM-MIT.
I STUDIED MY ASS OFF AND GOT ASSIGNED TO MY DREAM POST IN SECTION ONE, BUT THEN...
...I GOT PARTNERED WITH NUKARIYA-SAN...
...AND NOW MY CAREER'S A FIERY TRAIN WRECK.
AT FIRST, HE SEEMED NICE AND KIND OF EASYGOING. I THOUGHT I'D LUCKED OUT.
WHO'D HAVE THOUGHT HE IGNORES EVERYTHING THE HIGHER-UPS SAY...
AND YOUR POINT IS?
...DOES WHATEVER HE WANTS TO DO...
...AND IS THE BANE OF SECTION ONE!?
BOOO (DAAAZE)
NUKARIYA-SAN'S THE ONE WHO ORDERED THIS STAKEOUT TOO...
AHH...
IS IT GOING TO HAPPEN AGAIN?

!!
IS THE TOP BRASS GOING TO BLAME... ME...TOO...?

ZAZAAA (SKSHHHF)
DON (THUMP)
HUH.
GOSHI (WIPE)
WELL, THAT WAS PRETTY ENTERTAINING, BUT...
...WHAT REALLY GETS ME GOING...
...ARE HUMANS.
PASHIN (SHUT)
IT...HURTS...
MY HEAD...
...AND MY BODY...
...ARE BROKEN.

OW...
IT HURTS...
IT HURTS...
——AKIRA!
ZA (SHF)
ZA
ZA
......
WHAT THE... ARE YOU KIDDING ME?
THAT'S THE SAME BAT, ISN'T IT?
HOW DID IT FALL DOWN HERE ALL MANGLED!?

NO WAY A SIMPLE FALL...
...MESSED IT UP THIS MUCH...
YANA... GAWA?
HELLO?
SCREEN: CALLING...
NUKARIYA-SAN?
IT'S YANAGAWA.
BANNER: WHOLESALE GOODS
WE MAY BE ABLE TO HAUL IN THAT GUY OVER ANOTHER CHARGE.
BRING HIM IN FOR QUESTION-ING...
UM.
"ANIMAL ABUSE" WORKS, DOESN'T IT?
I CAN COME FORWARD AS A WITNESS.

オールドメモリアル センター
SIGN: OLD MEMORIAL CENTER
......!
WHAT THE HELL!? WHAT HAPPENED!?
THIS IS JUST ...!
ヒク
HIKU (TWITCH)
AKIRA...

I HAVE NO IDEA EITHER.
IT HURTS.
IT HURTS.
PAKU (GAWP)
ぱく
PAKU
ぱく
HELP ME.
I ONLY ASKED AL TO HELP OUT TWICE. ONCE TO GET A SKETCH OF THE PERP...
...AND ONCE TO FOLLOW THE BLOOD TRAIL.
HELP ME, AKIRA.
I HAD MY PARTNER WATCH THE PLACE. ACCORDING TO HIM...
EVERYTHING HURTS...
...AL CAME BY AROUND 9:00, AND...
WHY WOULD HE DO A...
OH!
...THING... LIKE...

I DON'T KNOW, BUT...
...AL MAY HAVE BEEN TRYING TO HELP, IN HIS OWN WAY.
I'M THE ONE WHO GOT HIM INVOLVED IN THIS.
I'M SORRY.
I TOOK HIM TO A VET, BUT THEY RECOMMENDED EUTHANIZING HIM.
BIKU (TWITCH)
BIKU
I DON'T REALLY UNDERSTAND HOW AL'S PHYSIOLOGY WORKS, SO...
BIKU
SO (STROKE)
LAST TIME...
...A HUMAN WOULD HAVE DIED FROM THE INJURIES HE HAD.
BUT...
...HE HEALED ON HIS OWN IN A COUPLE OF DAYS.
THAT MEANS HE'LL PROBABLY HEAL FROM THESE TOO IN TIME.

BUT...
...THIS IS JUST...
JUST LOOKING AT IT... HURTS...

IT'S ALMOST SUNSET.
IF HE TURNS HUMAN WHEN HE'S LIKE THIS...
SHU (SHUFF)
...WHAT'S GOING TO HAPPEN TO HIM!?

BIKU (TWITCH)
ビクッ
GUN (FOOM)
グーンッ
BORO (DANGLE)
ボロッ

ビクッ
BIKU
(TWITCH)
ビクーン
BIKUN
...SHIT.

KRIK
IT HURTS...
KRIK
I'M NOT... RECOVERING WELL...
KRIK
BIKU
BIKU
KRIK
KRIK
IT HURTS.
IT HURTS SO BAD...
KRIK
...I THINK I'M GONNA GO CRAZY!!
BIKU
HAAH!

GYAAAH!
AAAH!
AAAAAAH!
GAAAH!
AL!!
BORO (DRIP)
ぼろ
BORO
ぼろ

AKIRA...
AKIRA.
HFF!
HFF!
A...
HAH!
...KI...
HFF!
...RA...
WHAT IS IT?
WHAT ARE YOU TRYING TO SAY?
IN THE DES...
DESK...
BLOOD ...
HFF!

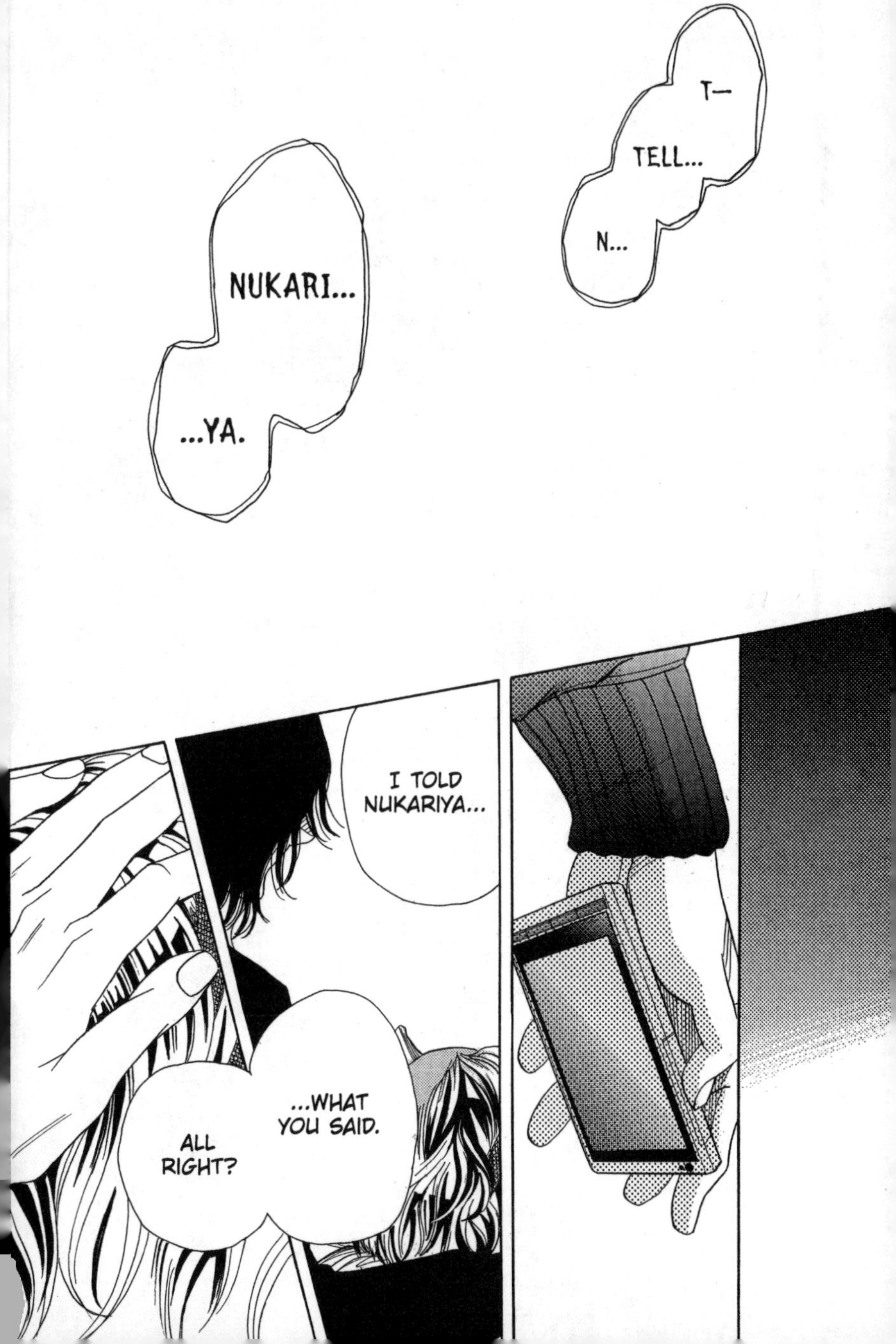
T— TELL... N...
NUKARI... ...YA.
I TOLD NUKARIYA...
...WHAT YOU SAID.
ALL RIGHT?

CAN YOU... WILL YOU REALLY RECOVER FROM THIS?
IT SEEMS LIKE YOU'D HEAL BETTER AS A HUMAN THAN A BAT, BUT...
...WHEN YOU GOT STABBED, THE WOUNDS CLOSED IN A NIGHT, AND THESE...
BIKUN (FLINCH)
BIKUN
EVERYTHING'S STILL WIDE OPEN.
IS IT BECAUSE THE WOUNDS ARE SO BIG?
BIKU
BIKU
PACHIN (SNAP)

MUA (WAFT)
むあっ
KUN (SNIFF)
くんっ
WH...
THAT'S...
WHAT?
HFF!
HFF!
AKIRA'S...
...BLOOD...

NO...
TA (PLIP)
たッ…
DON'T.
N...
NO.
NO...
... WANT ...
HAH!
HFF!
A... ...KI... ...RA...
... BLOOD ...
...NAS... ...TY.
FORGET THAT.

JUST DRINK.
しゅう
SHUU (FSSH)
しゅう…
SHUU

SHUU
しゅう
SHUU
しゅう
SHUU
しゅう
SHUU
しゅう

STOP RIGHT BEFORE I PASS OUT.
EXCEPT ...
...I GUESS YOU CAN'T HEAR ME.
AKIRA'S BLOOD...
...IS SO...
...SWEET.

KI (SCREECH)
BATAN (SLAM)
NUKA-RIYA-SAN!
YOU'RE LATE.
WE'RE HAVING A ROTTEN TIME KEEPING HIM AT THE STATION.
WE HAD TO FAKE A PAPERWORK ERROR.
THANKS TO THAT, EVEN THE COMMUNITY SAFETY DEPARTMENT IS MAD AT US.
...HM?
GLOVES!

...WHAT'S THIS?
DON'T TELL ME WE'RE GOING IN THERE.
DO WE HAVE A WAR-RANT?
OKAY, I WON'T TELL YOU.
HEY!
YOU'RE AT IT AGAIN, AREN'T YOU!?
SHUT UP.
I BET YOU HAVEN'T EVEN TOLD THE HIGHER-UPS!
LISTEN, DETECTIVE YANAGAWA.
THE BUILDING MANAGER IS WAITING IN FRONT OF THE GUY'S DOOR.
?
BY *SHEER COINCIDENCE*, THE FIRE ALARM WENT OFF BY MISTAKE.
AND SO...
...WE'RE USING A SPARE KEY TO ENTER THE APARTMENT OF A MAN WHO, *BY SHEER COINCIDENCE*, ISN'T HOME RIGHT NOW.
HUH?
BUT THAT'S... WHAT IF WE DON'T FIND PROOF?
WE CAN'T BE SURE THAT WE WILL.

I SWEAR.
EVERY SINGLE TIME...
YOU REALLY...
...NEVER STOP WHINING, DO YOU.
RAGE
オールド メモリアル センター
SIGN: OLD MEMORIAL CENTER
IS TAKA-TSUKA-SAN...
...GOING TO BE OKAY?

HE WENT TO THE HOSPITAL, GOT A BLOOD TRANSFUSION...
...THEN CAME BACK AND WENT STRAIGHT TO WORK ON A BODY BY HIMSELF.
THIS MORNING...
...WHEN HE CAME TO WORK LOOKING SO PALE, IT SCARED ME.
INSISTING HE CAN STILL DO WHAT'S ON HIS PLATE... HE WOULDN'T LISTEN.
HE MUST HAVE HAD A ROUGH TIME TAKING CARE OF AL YESTERDAY.
PATAN (SMACK)
I KNOW HE'S GOT IT ROUGH!!
BUT IF HE COLLAPSES...
...AND HAS TO BE TAKEN AWAY IN AN AMBULANCE, HE'LL JUST CAUSE MORE TROUBLE!!
IF HE'S FEELING UNWELL, HE COULD JUST LEAN ON ME INSTEAD OF PUSHING HIMSELF!

HE'S ALWAYS BEEN STUBBORN.
WANT SOME?
HE MAY BE CONCERNED ABOUT THE HOURS YOU WORK TOO.
SURE, ASSISTANTS ONLY WORK UNTIL FIVE O'CLOCK...
NO THANK YOU.
...BUT IN EXTRAORDINARY CIRCUMSTANCES LIKE THIS...!!
I BET...
...HE'S ON EDGE BECAUSE OF AL...
...AND HE COULDN'T HANDLE BEING AROUND SOMEBODY ELSE.
NGH!
TAKATSUKA-SAN SAID A DOG GOT HIM?
WANT SOME?
NO.
YEAH... HE SAID HE THINKS AL WILL HEAL UP SOON, BUT...
S—
SEEING HIM...
...LIKE THIS IS...
うるっ
URU (TEARY)
POOR LITTLE THING.
なで
NADE (STROKE)
IT JUST MAKES ME CRY.
BAN (BAM)

...YOU'RE STILL HERE?
IT'S PAST FIVE.
DID YOU ALREADY FINISH THAT BODY!?
BUT YOU ONLY STARTED A LITTLE BEFORE FOUR!
GUI (TUG)
THERE WAS NO RESTO-RATION WORK.
IT HADN'T BEEN THROUGH AN AUTOPSY EITHER.

DOSA (FWUMP)
PHEW...
SO.
HAS HE MOVED?
FURU (SHAKE)
FURU
NOT YET.
NOT AT ALL.
HAAH ...
......

JIRO (GLARE)
WHAT?
DO YOU NEED ME FOR SOME-THING?
HURRY UP AND GO HOME.

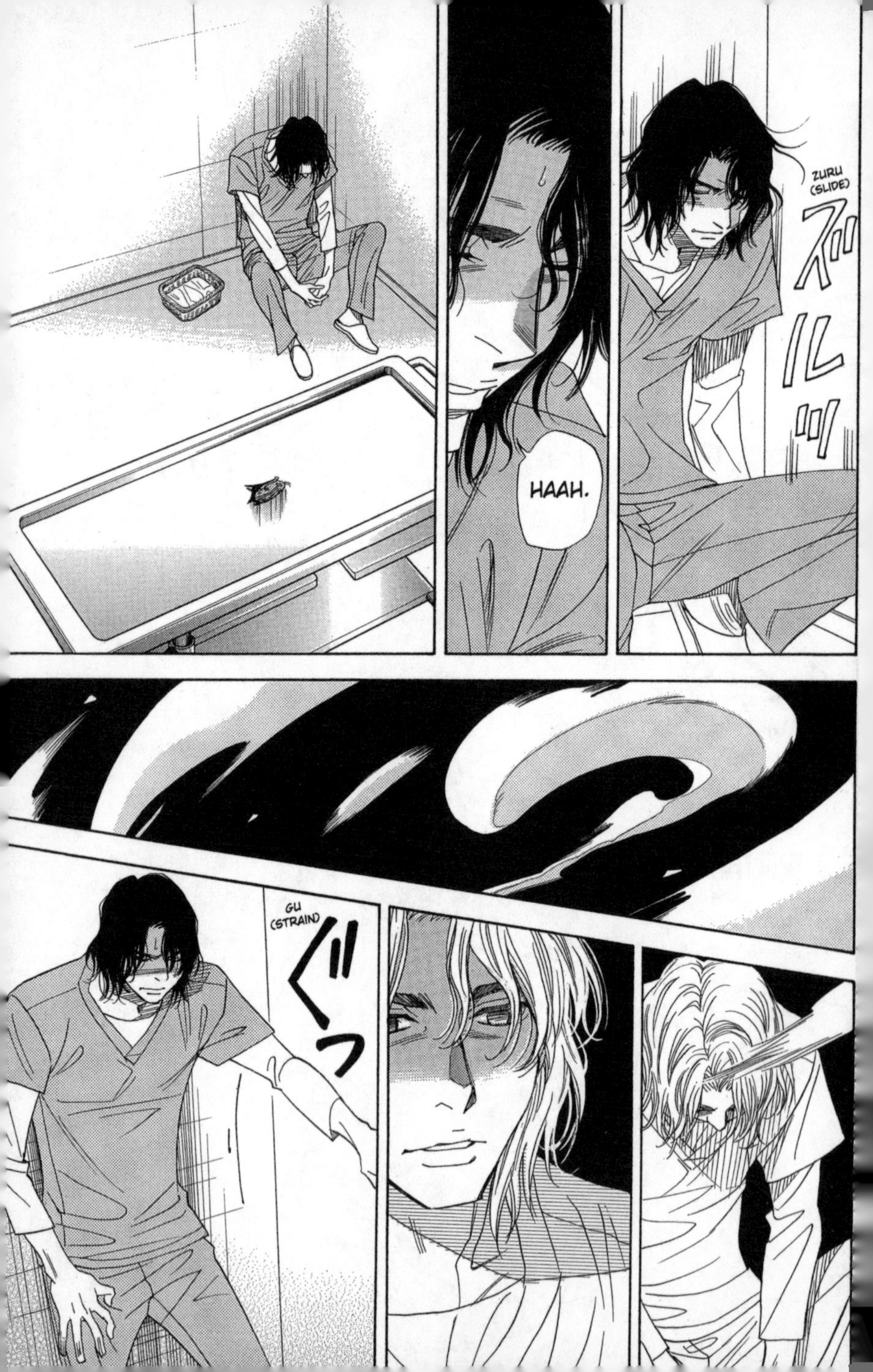
ZURU (SLIDE)
ズルッ
HAAH.
GU (STRAIN)
ぐっ

ドッ
DO (CLUNK)
AL.
DRINK.
......
はむ
HAMU (NOMF)

ちゅう
CHUU
ちゅう
ごく
CHUU (SLURP)
GOKU (GULP)
ごく
GOKU
ミチ
MICHI
ミチ
MICHI
ミチ
MICHI
ミチ
MICHI (KRIKL)
ミチッ
MICHI
OH...
I'M HEALING—
HEY.
YOUR COLOR'S LOOKING PRETTY GOOD.

WASHA (SHUFFA)
WASHA
わしゃ わしゃ
......
AKI RA.
HM?
ギ
GI (CREAK)
ト
TO (TMP)

ALL HEALED.

HUNH!?
YOU'RE BETTER!?
THAT BLOOD...
...HEAL MY BONES.
NO MORE...
...PAIN LEFT.
YOU WERE SO WEAK YOU COULDN'T EVEN SCREECH A MINUTE AGO!
HOW COULD YOU HEAL THAT EASILY!?
I'M SORRY.
クラ
KURAA (REEL)
あ
...HAAAH...
AKIRA?
DAMMIT... YOU'RE SO HEALTHY, IT'S ANNOYING.
IT ALL JUST HIT ME LIKE A TON OF BRICKS.
LET'S CLEAN THIS PLACE UP...
HARA はら
はら HARA (FRET)
...AND GO HOME. EVEN EATING SEEMS LIKE...

GURA (TOTTER)
...TOO MUCH ...
...WORK.
GASHI (GRAB)
FUWA (LIFT)

HEY!
WHA—!?
I CAN...
...WALK ON MY...
...OOOWN!
SHUTATA (DASHHH)
DON'T DO THINGS NOBODY ASKED YOU FOR!!

SU (SHF)
SU (SCOOT)
SU
SU
I AM SORRY.
PEKO (BOW)
THAT TICKS ME OFF.
TCH!
IF YOU'VE GOT THAT MUCH ENERGY, GO CLEAN UP THE CDC ROOM.
AND SOAK THE SUCTION BOTTLE YOU JUST DRAINED...
...IN DISINFECTANT.
OKAY.
KURU (TURN)
GACHA (KACHAK)

SASA (SWOOP)
さささっ
GHK!
WHOA!!
WHAT?
YOU HAVEN'T GONE HOME YET?
I FORGOT MY... PHONE...
UH... WHO'S THE GUY... BEHIND YOU?
THE PART-TIME JANITOR.
HE WAS CHANGING.
HE GOT THE WRONG ROOM.
HE'S, UM, NAKED...
HUH...? THE LOCKER ROOM'S NEXT DOOR.

I... SEE.
MAYBE IT'S NOT MY PLACE TO SAY THIS... BUT...
UM...
...I THINK IT WOULD BE BETTER TO KEEP YOUR WORK AND PRIVATE LIVES SEPARATE.
ALSO...
...PLEASE DON'T OVEREXERT YOURSELF TODAY. GO HOME AND REST UP.
PATAN (SHUT)

オールドメモリアル センター
SIGN: OLD MEMORIAL CENTER
A...
...KIRA.
AKIRA.
WE GO HOME.
NNGH...
AKIRA, YOU EAT.
IF NOT EAT, YOU GET WEAK.
葬祭会館
GO HOME, E AT DINNER.
...I FEEL SLUGGISH.
I'LL GO HOME AFTER I REST A LITTLE.
OH, THIS SOFA CONVERTS INTO A BED.
カチ
KACHI (CLICK)

KACHI KACHI
カチカチ
ドサ
DOSA (FWUMP)
YOU REST TOO.
AKIRA.
I NOT...
...DO MASSAGE TODAY.
語り
BUT I STILL...
...GET...
...BLOOD.
I AM...
...SORRY.
YOU DON'T HAVE TO APOLOGIZE TO ME.
YOU PROBABLY KNOW ALREADY, BUT HAVING YOU MASSAGE IS JUST A FORMALITY.

THE BLOOD WE TAKE FROM THE DEAD GETS DISINFECTED AND THROWN AWAY.
IT DOESN'T MATTER WHETHER WE TOSS IT...
...OR GIVE IT TO YOU.
TO PUT IT BLUNTLY.
ONLY...
...EVEN IF THAT'S SO...
とすん
TOSUN (THMP)
...THE PEOPLE GIVING IT TO YOU ARE HUMAN.
I WANTED TO MAKE SURE YOU FELT THAT.

STILL...
...YOU CAUSE ONE HELL OF A LOT OF TROUBLE.
I AM...
SHUN (DROOP)
しゅん…
... SORRY.
BUT...
...I'M GLAD...
...YOU'RE A VAMPIRE.

I'VE NEVER BEEN GLAD...
...I BECAME A VAMPIRE. NOT ONCE.
葬祭会館

ZZZ...
I WANT TO STAY WITH THIS GUY.

GOD...
...THANK YOU SO MUCH FOR LEADING ME...
...TO SOMEBODY KIND...
...IN THIS LAND ON THE FAR EDGE OF ASIA.

Breaking news.

速報
A man suspected in the serial murder spree...
...which occurred around Hachi●uji City...
王子連続殺人犯　逮捕
SCREEN: NEWS FLASH / HACHI●UJI SERIAL MURDERER ARRESTED
...has just been arrested.
PINPOOON (DING-DOOONG)

AL.
YOU'RE SURE THAT'S ALL YOU WANT?
I BOUGHT A LOT OF THEM, BUT...
...IT DOESN'T FEEL LIKE ENOUGH TO ME.
NUKARIYA, NOT YOUR FAULT.
NO WORRY.
GASA (RUSTLE)
GASA
GASA
I...
...WANTED THESE.
WHAT DID HE GIVE YOU?

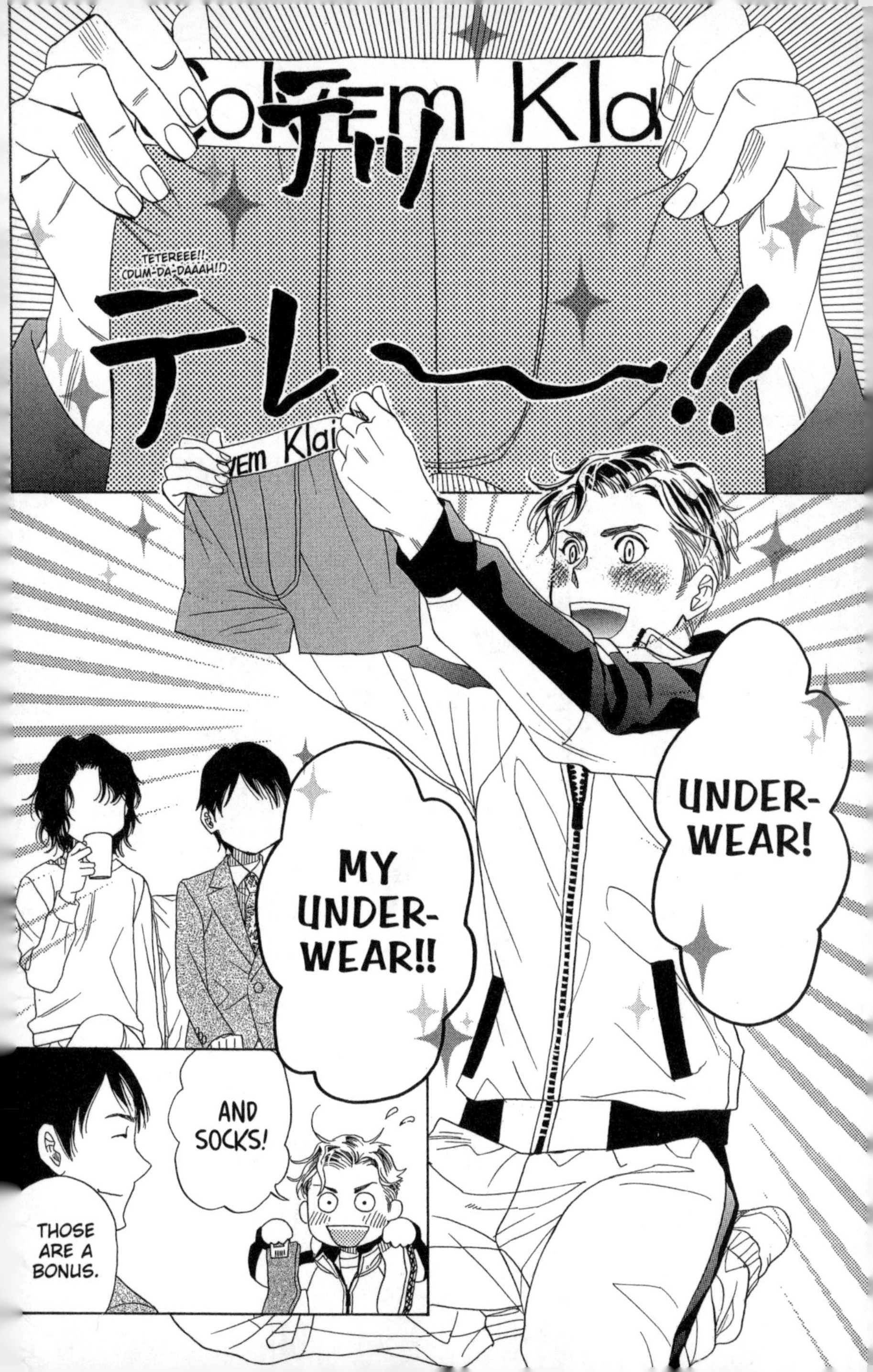
TETEREEE!!
(DUM-DA-DAAAH!!)
テレ〜〜!!
UNDER-WEAR!
MY UNDER-WEAR!!
AND SOCKS!
THOSE ARE A BONUS.

CLOTHES ARE ONE THING...
...BUT SERIOUSLY, SHARING UNDER-WEAR?
IF YOU WASH THEM, IT'S COMPLETLY SANITARY.
PON (POP)
KYU (SQUEAK)
KYU
BOXERS: AL
AKIRA. THIS MY UNDERWEAR.
DON'T WEAR. OKAY?
LIKE I WOULD!
I PUT THEM...
...IN CLOSET.
OKAY?
YOU CAN USE HALF OF THE LOWEST DRAWER.
JUST HALF, YOU HEAR?
YEAH!!

カチャ
KACHA (CHAK)
ぎゅ ぎゅ
GYU GYU (STUFF)
A DARK, BLACK CLOSET. LIKE AKIRA'S HAIR AND EYES.
SOMEDAY...
...IT WOULD BE GREAT IF ABOUT A THIRD OF IT...

...BECAME MY CLOTHES.
パタン...
PATAN (SHUT)

オールドメモリアル センター
SIGN: OLD MEMORIAL CENTER
TSUNO.
IT'S TIME. YOU CAN HEAD HOME.
HUH?
AT LEAST LET ME FINISH THIS REPORT.
I'LL WRITE IT.
UM...
TO—
SEE YOU GUYS LATER!
TODAY...
...LATER ON, IS *THAT* PART-TIMER...
...GOING TO BE HERE AGAIN...?
YES.
LISTEN.
IT SOUNDS LIKE YOU'VE GOT THE WRONG IDEA ABOU—
B—
BACK THERE...
...I WAS OUT OF LINE. I'M SORRY!!

IT'S TOTALLY FINE IF YOU SWING THAT WAY, TAKATSUKA-SAN.
I'M NOT PREJU-DICED!!
I MEAN IT, I SWEAR!! I JUST WANTED TO TELL YOU THAT!!
UH... LOOK ...
I DON'T "SWING THAT WAY."
BUT... BUT... HE WAS...
NAKED.
IT'S TRUE I'M NOT GREAT WITH WOMEN...
...BUT THAT DOESN'T MEAN I'M GAY.
......
I UNDER-STAND... MORE OR LESS.
AND WHAT DO YOU MEAN...
...BY "MORE OR LESS"?
...
JUST SPIT IT OUT!!

...TA—
TAKA-TSUKA-SAN...
YOU'RE "S," AREN'T YOU?
...I...
I AM NOT.
SOSO (SIDLE)
SURE.
IT'S REALLY OKAY.
WELL, I'M OFF.

WAIT.
IT'S FINE. REALLY.
I'M NOT!
GOOD GRIEF.
オールドメモリアルセンター
SIGN: OLD MEMORIAL CENTER
IT'S BEEN ONE DAMN THING AFTER ANOTHER, THANKS TO YOU.
WHAT ARE YOU GOING TO DO ABOUT IT?
HM?
......

A VAMPIRE AND HIS PLEASANT COMPANIONS② ◆ END

SKREE!
KYU (SQUEEZE)
きゅっ

IGNORANCE
しらぬが
IS BLISS
ほとけ
AL
ある
KATA
カタ
KATA (TAKKA)
I'M YANAGAWA.
カタカタ
カタカタカタ
KATA KATA
KATA KATA KATA KATA
RIGHT NOW...
...I'M BEING FORCED TO ORGANIZE A TON OF DOCUMENTS.
NUKARIYA-SAN IS MAD...
SKREE!
...I WATCHED THAT BAT GO INTO THE KILLER'S APARTMENT AND DIDN'T DO ANYTHING, OR SOMETHING LIKE THAT.
I FEEL...
...SO BAD FOR ME.

SOME-ONE ELSE
IF I'D BEEN ASSIGNED TO WORK WITH SOMEBODY ELSE, I (PROBABLY) WOULD BE THE BEST MAN ON THE FORCE, AND YET!!
DAMMIT! DAMMIT!
ARGH, ANOTHER MISTAKE! MAYBE IT'S A SOFTWARE GLITCH!
BREAK ROOM
とぽぽ
TOPOPO (TRICKLE)
STILL...
...I FIGURED YANAGAWA WOULD MAKE IT TOUGHER FOR NUKARIYA TO GO OFF THE RAILS, BUT...
...WITH ONE THING AND ANOTHER, THEY'RE...
...YOU KNOW—
"THE MASTER AND HIS HOUND."

AL
ある
Kawa ii
CUTE
OUT OF THE BLUE...
...NUKARIYA HAD A THOUGHT.
......
Akira— It's Nukariya. When you have a second, text me some photos of Al as a bat, please.
SEND
WHAT KIND OF BAT IS AL, ANYWAY?

MUUU (VRRR)
!!
THAT WAS WEIRDLY FAST.
He's right here. Will these work? —Akira
Could you send me some where his face is clearer?
SEND
MUUU
THAT DAY...
...NUKARIYA'S PHONE ACQUIRED A FOLDER LABELED "CUTE."
Apparently Maruyama made him a flower crown.

[Original Work] NARISE KONOHARA

A Vampire and His Pleasant Companions

[Art Staff] MORO-TAN · MIYA-SAN

KOMORING · AKAGAKI · OHNO

[Editor] SHIRAOKA [Manager] ANEJA

[Design] K. NAWATA

[Comics Editor] NORO (Gendai Shoin)

[Special thanks] [Original Work Editor] MIYAZAKI

......AND YOU!

Letters, please!

Attn: Marimo Ragawa

c/o Yen Press · 150 West 30th Street, 19th Floor · New York, NY 10001

Website: Crunchy Marimo Senbei http://www.ragawa.co.jp/

へり
SKREE!
ぽふんっ
はぐっ
ちょい ちょい
AAAAAAH

Translation Notes

COMMON HONORIFICS
no honorific: Indicates familiarity or closeness; if used without permission or reason, addressing someone in this manner would constitute an insult.
-san: The Japanese equivalent of Mr./Mrs./Ms. This is the fail-safe honorific if politeness is required.
-kun: Used most often when referring to boys, this honorific indicates affection or familiarity. Occasionally used by older men among their peers, but it may also be used by anyone referring to a person of lower standing.
-chan: Affectionate honorific indicating familiarity used mostly in reference to girls; also used in reference to cute persons or animals of any gender.
-sensei: A respectful term for teachers, artists, or high-level professionals.

CURRENCY CONVERSION
While exchange rates fluctuate daily, a good approximation is ¥100 to 1 USD.

PAGE 17
400 cc is 1.7 cups, just shy of a standard blood donation (one pint).

PAGE 89
Al is assisting with a very early step in the embalming process. After a corpse is washed, the limbs are massaged to "relax" stiffened joints and muscles.

PAGE 240
"S" as in "sadist," but the connotations in Japanese aren't as harsh as they are in English. Tsuno probably reached this conclusion because when he walked in on them, Al was naked and Akira wasn't, so he assumed it was a form of humiliation/domination play.

Please flip to back to read an exclusive, new short story.

The VAMPIRE & HIS PLEASANT COMPANIONS

MARIMO RAGAWA

ORIGINAL STORY NARISE KONOHARA

2

Translation: TAYLOR ENGEL   Lettering: ABIGAIL BLACKMAN

KYUKETSUKI TO YUKAI NA NAKAMA TACHI by MARIMO RAGAWA, NARISE KONOHARA

First published in Japan in 2017 by HAKUSENSHA, INC., Tokyo.
English translation rights arranged with HAKUSENSHA, INC., Tokyo through TUTTLE-MORI AGENCY, INC., Tokyo.

Yen Press
150 West 30th Street, 19th Floor
New York, NY 10001

Visit us at yenpress.com
facebook.com/yenpress
twitter.com/yenpress
yenpress.tumblr.com
instagram.com/yenpress

First Yen Press Edition: March 2021

Yen Press is an imprint of Yen Press, LLC.
The Yen Press name and logo are trademarks of Yen Press, LLC.

The publisher is not responsible for websites (or their content) that are not owned by the publisher.

Library of Congress Control Number: 2020946726

ISBNs: 978-1-9753-2062-1 (paperback)
978-1-9753-2063-8 (ebook)

10 9 8 7 6 5 4 3 2 1

BVG

Printed in the United States of America

Akira had absolutely no interest in the acting profession. The man who was helping him out here in America worked in the film industry and kept asking Akira to appear in films, but Akira stubbornly refused.

He didn't understand what drove people to invest their money and their lives in imaginary worlds. That said, as an aspiring embalmer, a professional dedicating to keeping the dead looking beautiful, he might qualify as a denizen of a fictional world himself.

"By the way, what field are you planning to go into?"

Nukariya looked back and smiled.

"I'm going to be a detective."

The guy might be hard to pin down, but his future goal was extremely solid.

"Your acting was pretty impressive."

"I, um… I haven't been to a…"

"Akira."

With perfect timing, Nukariya rejoined them. Akira handed the camera to its owner.

"That guy came to return this."

"Oh, sorry for the trouble. Thank you."

While Nukariya thanked the guy, Akira made a quick exit. As he caught up to him, Nukariya groused, "I'm sorry I kept you waiting, but there's no need to hurry off like that."

When he glanced back, the brunette was grilling the blond guy. He had returned the camera, so Akira had figured he'd repay him by lying about meeting at a film shoot. Would the possibility that the guy might actually have acted in a movie make the girl less condescending?

…Pointless. I did something pointless. I'm not going to think about it anymore.

"Wait a minute."

Nukariya stopped him in front of an ice cream stand. Akira had no choice but to wait, and his classmate returned with ice cream for two.

"I'm glad we got the camera back," Nukariya said, licking his ice cream.

"I'd heard if you lost things over here, you'd never see them again. That blond guy seemed pretty decent—and he was handsome."

"I'm not a fan of westerners."

"You've got a pretty dramatic face yourself, Akira."

Akira turned back, glaring at him, but Nukariya was nonchalant. "Hey, it's the truth.

"It sounded like that guy is trying to break into acting. When I went back to get the camera, he was pitching himself to that red-haired scout who flagged you down. He said he'd play any role, things like that. I couldn't bring myself to interrupt, so I was watching them from a distance, but then a Japanese couple asked me for directions. While I was helping them, I lost sight of him."

"Oh, Al."

The girl with chestnut hair called out to the young guy.

"Didn't you have a meeting to get to?"

There was a trace of derision in her voice.

"Um… Yeah, but…I'm looking for somebody. You haven't seen a pair of Chinese guys around here, have you—"

The young guy made eye contact with Akira and came running over, his mouth still half-open. His shining blond hair was rumpled, and he paused, looking troubled.

"This guy's probably not going to understand English, though."

He'd said just what he was thinking, without censoring himself.

"What do you want?"

"Whoa!" The guy jerked back, startled. But, recovering, he said, "I wanted to give this back. It's your friend's, isn't it?" He held out the camera. Nukariya had gone off to find this guy, but apparently they'd managed to miss each other.

When Akira took it, the man put a hand to his chest in relief. "I'm glad I got it back to you." He'd actually come looking for them so he could return it. *What a nice guy.*

Akira examined the man's face. In his practicals at school, he was studying plastic surgery and makeup. Looks didn't interest him. However, although the man's features weren't bad, his overall appearance seemed rather rough, unpolished, and rustic.

"Are you traveling together? You had all sorts of photos on there."

"You looked at the camera roll?"

The man mumbled an excuse. "Just—just a little. The thing is, I've never been anywhere except the state where I was born and California. Are you here from China?"

The girl with chestnut hair was watching them steadily. Was this the lying show-off the girls had been talking about? The self-proclaimed "actor"? Even if he was, he didn't seem to be a bad guy.

"We met at that film shoot, didn't we?"

He spoke loudly on purpose. The brunette was listening to them.

"Huh? Uh…"

The guy was bewildered.

"Jahne, Jahne! That friend of yours was really cool! And he's an actor? That's amazing! Give me his number, okay?"

Two girls, one blonde, the other brunette, were talking a short distance away. The blonde's voice was unpleasantly loud.

"You mean Al? Oh, him. He's nobody."

The girl with chestnut hair, who was fiddling with her phone, jerked her chin.

"Aha. I knew it. I'd heard he was going to college in Nebraska, so I thought it was weird for him to be acting in Hollywood all of a sudden. I just texted a friend over there and asked, and apparently he models for flyers quite a lot, but as far as anyone knows he's never been in a movie or on TV. With his personality, I bet he'd be bragging about it to anybody who'd listen if he'd actually landed a part."

"You mean..."

"He was lying to make himself look good. Either that, or maybe he thinks being an extra is 'acting.' Super-obvious lies like that are so lame."

The girl with chestnut hair snapped her phone shut and sighed.

"Since I came here, I've run into tons of guys who called themselves 'actors,' and none of them was any good. They think if they say they're in show business, it doesn't matter if they're earning zilch and you'll forgive them for being broke. That spoiled mindset is seriously irritating. Unsuccessful actors are just blue-collar workers anyway."

Akira had zero interest in the entertainment industry, and he completely agreed with what the girl was saying, but the arrogant way she said it irked him.

"He's pretty handsome, though. He might actually end up famous one of these days."

The blonde sounded hopeful, and the brunette laughed at her.

"Sure, maybe. But there's probably about as much chance of finding gold dust in the river, don't you think?"

"Say, Jahne? Isn't that him?"

The blonde pointed across the street. A young guy in a cap was looking around anxiously. That flashy shirt seemed familiar... Was that the guy Nukariya had asked to take their picture in front of that mural?

guy still has my camera; I forgot to get it back. Wait here."

Nukariya started back the way they'd come. Akira had always thought the guy was shrewd and hard to pin down, and he'd watched him win people over before you could blink, but during the past two years, Nukariya had leveled up even further.

After graduating from high school, Akira had come to America to study embalming and enrolled at a mortuary science college in California. Both the lectures and the practicals were tough, on top of which he really wasn't used to English. The days were a hectic blur, and for the first few months he hadn't even had the time to sleep properly. Only after a year and a half did Akira finally have enough leeway to put down the textbooks and nap for a few hours on the weekends.

As if he'd been waiting for Akira's schedule to relax, his high school classmate Nukariya had come to America on summer vacation by himself. He hadn't contacted Akira ahead of time. Akira had been giving his lab partner Pat a ride home after Pat's car broke down. When he stopped at a diner on the return trip, he ran into Nukariya by sheer coincidence.

"Hey, if it isn't Akira!"

Due to the good looks he'd inherited from his mother, Akira had been picked up and scouted countless times; as stuff like that annoyed him, he invariably ignored it. He only turned to look on this occasion because the voice had sounded familiar and because the words had been spoken in Japanese.

His classmate, whom Akira hadn't seen in a year and a half, said he wanted to go to Hollywood & Highland—a disgustingly mainstream, typical tourist trap—and asked Akira to show him around. He hadn't been able to turn Nukariya down, and now here they were. He wanted to get out of this shallow place ASAP, but Nukariya was taking his time coming back. The idea of going home on his own did cross Akira's mind, but just walking ahead a little had been enough for Nukariya to accuse him of leaving him behind. Pressing his lips together in irritation, Akira decided to tough it out and wait.

Someone grabbed Akira Takatsuka's arm from behind. He was about to shake himself free—violently, if necessary—but the individual who was doubled over, panting for breath, wasn't the middle-aged redheaded man with the crude face. It was his former classmate, Nukariya.

"D-don't leave me behind! That was mean."

"I can't stand guys like him."

"Yes, but my English isn't that good, you know."

Nukariya, catching his breath at last, put his hands on his hips. "Honestly...whether you liked it or not, it was pretty clear that he was scouting you. You could have turned him down properly. Walking off without saying anything was plain insulting."

"I don't need to be polite to people who are rude enough to flag me down on the street."

"It's not 'being polite,' it's just basic manners."

No matter what Akira said, his friend responded calmly and with good arguments. Intensely irritated, Akira spread his arms wide.

"I didn't want to come to a tourist trap like this in the first place! You were the one who said you wanted to see the Hollywood Theatre while you were in L.A., so I went out of my way to bring you here, remember? You're not even in the movie business. Why bother visiting a thing like that!? I don't get it."

"You're missing the point of sightseeing, Akira. Actually *looking* at things you'd normally never have a chance to see is the whole point."

"Mr. Literal over here..."

"It's hardly worth getting so upset over—oh, crud. That blond

This story is set in America, back when Albert Irving was still a normal human, a teenager with big dreams of becoming an actor.

It happened long before Akira Takatsuka, a college student training to become an embalmer, met Al, an imperfect, failed vampire who would find himself shipped to Japan as a frozen bat...

A VAMPIRE AND HIS PLEASANT COMPANIONS SHORT STORY

AKIRA TAKATSUKA, TWENTY YEARS OLD

Narise Konohara